PR MAGNET

Create Best-Selling Books and Attract Free Radio Interviews

By
Debbi Dachinger
and
Viki Winterton

PR MAGNET:
Create Best-Selling Books and Attract Free Radio Interviews
©2016 by Debbi Dachinger and Viki Winterton

Expert Insights Publishing
8640 University City Blvd., Suite A-3 #247
Charlotte, NC 88312

All rights reserved. No part of this book may be reproduced in any manner whatsoever, nor may it be stored in a retrieval system, transmitted, or otherwise copied for public or private use, without written permission other than "fair use" as brief quotations embodied in articles and reviews.

ISBN-13: 978-1541048546
ISBN-10: 1541048547

15 14 13 12 11   1 2 3 4 5

A portion of the profits from this book will be donated to International Animal Rescue Organization. "At International Animal Rescue we do exactly what our name says – we save animals from suffering around the world. Our work includes cutting free and caring for dancing bears in India, rescuing primates from captivity in Indonesia and sterilizing and vaccinating stray dogs and cats in developing countries. Wherever possible we return rescued animals to their natural environment but we also provide a permanent home for animals that can no longer survive in the wild."
https://www.internationalanimalrescue.org/

Dedication

Massive gratitude to our students and coaching clients, who have attended and learned in our workshops, private consulting sessions, done for you programs and teleseminars, and then gone out in the world to become successful authors and radio personalities.

In addition, we thank those clients and friends who have entrusted us to turn their books into bestsellers, and their messages into exquisite radio interviews.
In essence, they all embraced the knowledge and opportunity and became PR Magnets.

And to you, dear reader, now that you have picked up this book, we hope that after reading it you will also choose to step up your book and business, and utilize media for the magic and positive change it will create for you.

Endorsements

"A refreshingly practical and brilliant book for those wanting to create a bigger impact. This well written book is an important resource for today's business people and entrepreneurs. You will find this read to hold several important, but seldom talked about, issues and techniques for creating word of mouth epidemics around your book and your work. To beginners and advanced alike, I highly recommend reading this book to learn how to propel your message and business out in a free and big way using these PR industry secrets." ~ **Teresa de Grosbois,** President, Wildfire Workshops Inc.

"*PR Magnet*, Debbi Dachinger and Viki Winterton's new book is an invaluable guide for anyone writing or planning to write a book. It is a soup-to-nuts strategic plan for turning your book into a bestseller—loaded with practical tips and insights, gathered from the authors' decades of experience. As a 35-year veteran of Washington news reporting, I've been pitched in lots of ways and as the author of four versions of *Find It Online*, I've also been through the paces of book promotion. I especially love some of the book's useful nuggets like cleaning up your social media profile before pitching yourself; remembering the radio show you're trying to get on is not all about you; and making sure you speak in 'bites not in meals.' *PR Magnet* is the how-to manual to use to turn your book into a bestseller." ~ **Alan Schlein**, runs DeadlineOnline.com, author of the bestselling *Find It Online* books, CEO of SmartGuide.Solutions

"*PR Magnet* is an incredible tool for taking you and your message from idea and finessing it and you into a well sought after virtuoso. When you start with the cornerstone of messaging your brilliance correctly, the life you build reflects your core expertise, affecting every aspect of your world. Your health, wealth, and profession will benefit, helping you maximize results and create positive change." ~ **Natalie Ledwell**, Best-Selling Author and Co-Founder of Mind Movies LLC

"I decided 2017 would be the year I would write the book my clients have been clamoring for—a guide book for solving their specific problems. But where to start? I got my hands on Debbi Dachinger's and Viki Winterton's brand new book, **PR MAGNET:** *Create Best-Selling Books and Attract Free Radio Interviews*. It surprised me. Over the years, I've taken many writing and publishing courses and they've left me more confused than clear. THIS book by Debbi and Viki is a revelation. It is a clear, step-by-step guide for creating a book that gets published, purchased and noticed in an increasingly crowded marketplace. For me personally, it's an answer to a prayer because I love having a strategy or formula to apply by someone who has already succeeded. I'm able to pour my own unique point of view, philosophy and expertise into this formula so I don't have to start at zero or miss steps... I don't like missing steps and then having to redo things a bunch of times. No more guess work and no more fumbling around looking for guidance. I'm excited to refer to this book again and again in publishing my next book. It's a coach in a book. Thank you, Debbi and Viki, for taking the time to share your expertise and the PRECISE DETAILS of what a successful book requires!" ~ **Baeth Davis**, PalmReadingPro.com

"If you want to help people with your business, then people must know you exist and what you do. There is a formula for success in the world of PR, media interviews and bestsellers and in this book, Debbi Dachinger and Viki Winterton share their tried and true systems. Whether you are a speaker, author, entrepreneur or global leader, this excellent book gives fresh, hot tips toward a magnetic and noble cause."
~ **Orna Walters**, Co-Founder, www.CreatingLoveOnPurpose.com

"Have you seen those authors who seem to be everywhere? Do you wonder how they got there? Debbi Dachinger and Viki Winterton have taken the guesswork out of how to become a best-selling author; they provide step-by-step instructions on how to get there by becoming a *PR Magnet*! This is an attractively presented book full of practical wisdom on radio, how to be interviewed, the afterlife of a book, how to do press, and how to message yourself in media for big results!" ~ **Michelle Colon-Johnson,** Founder of 2 Dream Productions, Inc., Making Authors Successful At Selling Their Books

"Debbi and Viki each have decades of experience in book publishing and media. Best of all they are not only masters at what they do, but also able to teach their winning strategies in a clear, effortless fashion. This easy-to-read, conversational book is packed with invaluable information, helping you elevate your business step-by-step. If you are looking to expand your reach through bestselling books and remarkable radio results, this is the book to read. I recommend it highly!" ~ **Zsuzsa Novak**, Global Impact Expert

Table of Contents

Introduction..8

1. Publishing and the Press.................................11
   Navigate Today's Innovative Landscape

2. Your Book..31
   Pave a Smooth Journey for Your Book

3. Your Book Promotion......................................59
   Elevate Huge Book Promotion Success

4. Your Book Launch...91
   Propel Your Book to Success

5. Your Press and Media Relations..........................129
   Ace Your PR Skills

6. Your Radio Broadcast....................................165
   Book Yourself Busy on Radio Shows

7. Your Interviews...203
   Professional Secrets to Lucrative Interviews

8. Beyond Your Book..221
   Skyrocket Your Success

   About the Authors.......................................250

   Resources...254

Introduction

Bestseller books and radio—two of today's most powerful mediums, if you know how to use them!

Meet Viki Winterton and Debbi Dachinger, two experts who have come together to collaborate on this book and take you on a journey to discover how to become a best-selling author and PR radio magnet. They admire and respect one another's work. This is actually very rare; they are <u>both</u> experts in publishing and also in radio broadcast.

Viki is the founder of Expert Insights Publishing and Write Now Radio, a #1 international best-selling author, a global radio host, and an award-winning publisher. Viki is a speaker who has addressed crowds numbering from the dozens to those numbering in the thousands, and a coach to global Fortune 100 companies and solopreneurs. She is dedicated to helping over 1,000 authors to date build their platform and publish their book to bestseller with the utmost of integrity. Viki founded an eight-figure ad agency in her mid-20s, and created 25 years of worldwide coaching success with Fortune 100 companies and entrepreneurs. In the last five years, Viki has also created two global coaching and writing networks, two broadcast shows, three award-winning magazines, and Expert Insights Publishing—home of best-selling books, where visionaries and those on the rise come together to create immediate impact.

Debbi Dachinger is a Media Personality who produces and hosts "Dare to Dream," a syndicated, award-winning radio; is a red carpet correspondent, international #1 best-selling author, frequent interview guest, speaker, and certified consultant/coach of Media Makeovers for Global messengers. Debbi helps leaders and change-makers clarify and deepen their message to articulate who they are and what they do, with big results. She mentors authors, healers, spiritual teachers, transformational leaders and global messengers on how to market themselves through media, networking and those they connect with to bring in clients, followers, and sales, and to fill up workshops. She is known as an expert on both sides of the microphone (as a host and as an interview guest), and on both sides of the pen (as an author and as a mentor to authors).

How do you write and promote a best-selling book? How do you attract media? How do you get asked on radio? How do you interview elegantly in order to receive return engagements? The benefits are astounding, but where do you start? The latest statistics show there are about 11,000 business books published every year in the US, that doesn't even include self-published print or e-books, of which there are tens of thousands, increasing exponentially every year. So the question is: How are you going to distinguish your book so that it's published, purchased, and noticed? How is it going to stand out in this crowded marketplace?

In this book, you will discover how to get known as the expert, how to get your book done easily, how you can make big money before you write a word, and how you can bridge the gap between publishing and promoting your work to bestseller and beyond.

Once you know how, just a few of the benefits are: Generating more leads, closing more deals, charging higher fees, and starting your speaking career or getting better speaking engagements. Actually publishing a book propels you into getting known as an expert in your field, brings your business credibility, and provides brand clarity and distinction. Your book is going to benefit you and your business in a host of ways, but writing it is just the beginning—about 5% of the work. The other 95% focuses on promoting your book. So say "Yes!" to becoming a bestseller and a radio PR magnet, married together in this book—your formula for success!

Chapter One
Publishing and the Press
Navigate Today's Innovative Landscape

DEBBI: Welcome and congratulations on your decision to become a best-selling author and radio PR magnet. We are two experts who have come together to write this book. We admire and respect each other's work. This is a unique opportunity for you in that we are both experts in the publishing/self-publishing world and also experts in radio.

Viki will be sharing wisdom in self-publishing, and I will cover a vast amount of information in radio media. If you don't know Viki yet, it is my profound pleasure to introduce you to her. Viki is the founder of Expert Insights Publishing and Write Now radio. She is a #1 best-selling author, global radio host, award-winning publisher, and the founder of the award-winning *PUBLISHED!* Magazine. She has also taken over one thousand authors from around the world to bestseller status.

I am Debbi Dachinger, a media personality. I host and produce the syndicated, award-winning radio show called "Dare to Dream," interview in front of the television camera, interview celebs on the red carpet. I am a live stream event host, a presentation speaker, and have written best-selling books. I'm a certified coach with clients worldwide who seek my technical expertise in success and radio/book media.

Viki Winterton and Debbi Dachinger: we are your experts.

In this chapter, you will learn how you can get known as the expert, how to get your book done easily, how you can make big money before you even write a word, and how you can bridge the gap between publishing and promoting your book. We will entrust you with many treasured success secrets.

We will also cover how to attract media, how to get asked to do radio interviews, and how to do so elegantly with some of my personal interview power tips. There are tremendous benefits to reaching the radio listening audience.

YOUR BESTSELLER OVERVIEW

I love statistics. Statistics are meaningful to me. I am a bit of a researcher.

There is a gentleman by the name of Jack Covert. He is the CEO of **800 CEO READ**. The latest statistic is there are about eleven thousand business books published every year in the United States. That does not include self-published, print, or e-books. There are tens of thousands of books for sale, and that number is increasing exponentially every year. So the question is always, how are you going to distinguish your book so it is published, so it is purchased, so it is noticed? How is it going to stand out from the competition, and what are the benefits of making that happen?

For authors who publish their books and do semi well to very good, there are benefits of generating more leads, closing more deals, charging higher fees, getting better speaking gigs or starting to get speaking engagements. Other benefits to publishing a book include personal credibility, business credibility and brand clarity. So the point is if you have a book in you, writing it is going to benefit you and your business in a host of ways. Always remember, writing is just the beginning. That's the 5%, and then there is the 95%—focusing on selling your book. The more promotion you do, the more you will see a return on your investment. So becoming a best-selling author and being a radio PR magnet are married together.

Viki, what are some of the chronic issues for authors? What are some of the mistakes that authors make?

VIKI: Debbi, I really appreciate you asking this. I was an entrepreneur from birth. My Father was a barnstormer and I think I came by it genetically. I started an ad agency when I was in my mid-twenties and we did eight figures within three years. We were acquired and that parlayed into a coaching career. For over thirty years, I travelled all over the world and helped CEOs of Fortune 500 companies define their vision, and then assisted their teams in making that vision a reality. I became travel weary and decided to open an online community and give back to the coaching world. I was approached about writing a book. I had done all of these things and when someone asked me about writing a book, I just froze up.

I became fearful of the entire concept. I was frightened about how much there was to do and whether or not what I had to say was valuable, despite a well-rounded and accomplished background in business. This still just stopped me in my tracks. I wanted to share this with you because I think a lot of us feel this way. Or we may start a book and get stuck. It can seem so complicated, and in some ways it is.

So that we all have a good understanding of what this kind of project requires, here are some of the steps of getting a book written and published.

First of all, you have to have a concept. It needs to be a good or unique concept, or unique angle on what may be already out there.

Then you need to write the book. You have to have a catchy **title** and a **subtitle** that explains what people are going to experience as benefits when they read your book.

Then you need a **cover** design that will really knock the socks off readers—something that will truly attract them.

Most books have **Introductions** and **Forewords**. Finding a popular celebrity or a well-known expert to write your foreword, and then getting other experts to endorse your book can be challenging. If you can do it, however, it will be worth it.

Then, you need to have your book professionally **edited**. This is really important and not inexpensive. When we publish a book for ourselves or other writers, we go through three different editing processes with editors who specialize in different aspects of editing. It is critical that your book represent you well from the stand point of editing.

Next, you have to evaluate **publishing strategies** and decide whether or not you want to go the traditional route or self-publish, if you need to find an agent, and if you need promotional support for your book. Do you have enough joint venture partners or a strong network to make this happen yourself? Do you have time to develop this?

Last, you need to establish a robust PR and **promotional strategy.** This is critical to the success of your book because writing it, once again, is only 5%. The promotion around it is what really makes things happen. It is important to mention that if you should decide to go the traditional publishing route, it takes anywhere from eighteen months to three years to get published. They do not help you with the promotion of your book. They expect you to come to them with a promotional plan in place. Your marketing preparedness is one of the parameters on which they judge whether or not they will actually publish your book.

So these days, all of this is expected from you. It was not always this way, but it is now. There are very few publishers out there that will even touch the promotion of your book. At Expert Insights Publishing, we developed programs where we do this. The reason we even started offering the service was because we saw that this was an area of tremendous need and very few were providing bestseller promotion at a reasonable fee. At the time of this writing, we have taken over one thousand authors to bestseller status.

So let's focus for a moment on self-publishing. These days, unless you are absolutely set on having a traditional publishing house handle your work, self-publishing has many advantages.

First of all, you can turn a self-published book around as fast as you can write it. It is just that simple to make it happen. You can do it yourself and get all the royalties from all of your book sales. You can use the book in any way you like. Some publishing houses will even require "right of first refusal" for future books. When you publish your book yourself, you have total control over your book and royalties, so it is a really wonderful, creative world.

Some people will ask if anyone can publish a book. I compared this to when I started my advertising agency at twenty-four years old. At that age, I had been modeling for a living, and I had no idea how to do any of what was required to develop an ad agency business. I was on the other side of the camera and the business. To begin, I developed some really good people around me. I hired people to help me with the things that I didn't know how to do, and to train me on how to do the things I was interested in doing. So, if you have a passionate spirit about getting your book done, you can fill in the blanks for anything you need by surrounding yourself with the right people. You can pay for services like ghost writing if you get stuck or you feel that you need help with the actual writing of your book.

I know that Debbi and I both personally feel that everyone has a story in them that needs to be told—perhaps more than one! Author Joan C. King, a good friend of mine who is no longer with us, was also a neuroscientist and an unbelievable coach who traveled all over the world. She told me one time that not only is it a privilege to be able to tell your story, it is your obligation to the world. If you don't tell your special and unique story, you leave a hole in the world, because no one can tell your story like you can tell it. Even if it is subject matter that is already out there and scores of people are talking about it, no one is going to be able to tell your story the way you do. There are people out there in the world that need to hear your story just the way only you tell it.

So it is really important to overcome any fear, any challenges that you have about getting your story out there. Not only can your book add value to your business like nothing I have ever seen, it can change the lives of those throughout the world who read your book. I was in the advertising, promotion and process reengineering world for many, many years. I have never seen anything in my entire career that changes lives of authors like a book, changes businesses like a book, nor changes the lives of readers like a book. It gives you instant credibility and it is the most powerful vehicle that you can possibly have working for you. I really want to stress the importance of having the ability to overcome anything that is holding you back that may look bigger than life to you now.

The second point that Debbi made that I would really like to speak to is how you can make really big money if you have just started the journey and before you write a single word. The most important thing that you can do early on is develop your book cover.

Do readers and people judge a book by its cover? You bet they do! We all do! So it is extremely important that you have a powerful cover because of what you can do with that book cover. Once your cover is developed, even if you are not planning to write your book for a year or more, that book cover can do wonders for you and your business right now, today! You don't have to wait. As I mentioned, you don't even have to have one word written.

Since this is so important, let's spend just a little time going over the importance of the different components of a book cover. As I mentioned earlier, the book cover really needs to grab the reader's attention. If you're using it for promotional purposes and an introduction to open doors and opportunity for you long before your book is done, you want your book cover to represent you well.

If you put yourself in the readers' place when you are making your final decision for your book's title, it will help you ask the right questions, like, does this make sense to the reader? Will it be easy for someone to recall it? To remember it? Does it convey the message that I want to convey? Will it supply the readers with clarity about the intention and content of the book?

Once you decide on the book title, be sure to buy that domain name. I would go so far as to say continue to work that title until you have one that has the domain name available. It is that important because you never know where your book is going to go. You want to own the rights to your title. Think beyond the .com and consider all of the extensions that go with your book as far as your platform. You may want to build classes based on the title of that book. You may want to build coaching courses, private classes, masterminds, and group classes. You may want to start a web TV show.

You may want to develop speaking engagements based on the book title, so you want to be sure you own the domain. You can simply go to www.godaddy.com where it costs less than ten dollars to buy most domains.

The title should not be more than four or five words. The shorter, the better, but it does need to convey a powerful message. Your subtitle can be longer, can define your title further, and can sell the benefit of the book to the reader. You want to make sure it includes a key word that may not be in your title that people may be searching for on the web. You want to use a large, readable font for the title, and a slightly smaller, but readable font for subtitle. Place the subtitle beneath the title on the cover image.

Contrasting color tones are great to incorporate, but remember that your book cover may be displayed in places that are only black and white. I suggest that when you design your cover, keep in mind what it will look like in black and white because it needs to work for both if you're really going to use your book cover to the maximum potential.

Choose a strong image. I just had a book that went bestseller last year called *Beyond Your Book*. The cover image had pages flying off the book, and it was all done very dramatically in black and white. Debbi's book, *Dare to Dream: This Life Counts*! was based on her Dare to Dream radio show, and she has her image on the book's cover. It's very distinctive and really attracts the eye. So you need to find a strong image that will do that for you. You need to include your name at the bottom of the cover, and if you have other titles that you would like to share with future readers, it gives you credibility to do so, so by all means, do.

On most of my books, I state that I am an Award-Winning Publisher, and #1 International Best-Selling Author. Again, this helps build credibility for those who are thinking of buying the book.

These are just a few of my favorite tips, and I hope you find them helpful when you are developing your cover. Now I am going to go into a few things on how you can use your book cover, even before you start writing a single word in your book. These tips can magnify your presence and enforce the fact that you are an expert in your field. You can get potential PR gigs, as well as TV and radio appearances.

One of our authors was actually on *The Today Show*. He secured his interview on the show with a book cover for a future book around the subject matter that he thought was very topical, saying that the book would soon be released. This is really very powerful.

We discussed a rather long list of requirements to make a book happen. Team up with someone who can help you. We have services that we offer to authors at every stage in their book and there are all sorts of people out there that can help you if you get stuck. It could be a publicist; it could be an editor. For some things on that list that you are not comfortable with, you can always hire people. You can sometimes get a discount or do a trade when you bring people on to help you and offer to mention them as an acknowledgement in your book. You can always barter and negotiate with them.

You can promote your book with current tools. I cannot tell you how important and easy this is. You can put your book cover on your business card saying "soon to be released" or "coming soon." Include your book cover in the signature of all of your emails.

The release of your upcoming book can be a signature line for everything you do on the web. Where appropriate, get that book cover out there and let people know what you are doing. Whether you are doing a press release, a report or anything else, if you have that book cover and say that you have a book coming out soon, this is going to be a tremendous attraction for people to want to work with you. I highly encourage this. It doesn't cost much to do and it is sitting there waiting for you right now.

Be helpful, and every chance you get to answer questions, refer to wisdom in your book. It is important to bring your book into conversation because again, it presents you as an expert. You are getting people interested in talking about your book well before it ever comes out.

Highlight your achievements. As we mentioned, definitely highlight them on the book cover and also highlight your achievements when you meet people in your conversation. Anytime you mention the book, be sure to talk about any awards you received, and so forth. If you are at a place where you have no awards yet, think about the different aspects of expertise that you have developed around your subject matter and be sure to bring them up. When you are humble, you may not be giving people the information they need to determine how much they want to do business with you. It is actually cheating them. Look at providing information about your expertise as a benefit for those people who you are serving.

It helps to build a story around your book. Share stories about how the book developed and what created the subject matter for you, and make it realistic. Share your book's stories on social media, too. It is really important that people can relate you as a person. It is your human circumstance, your human story and ways you can share it that will endear you to your followers. It will create a sense of your vulnerability when you are able to reveal this and speak to how it touched you. It is really important that you do this on social media, and it is important that you do this when you blog and write articles related to the content of your book.

I read a story one time about a coach who lost his sister when a car rolled over her. I had always looked at him as a very untouchable expert, a very well-known entity out there in the world. When he talked about the feelings and the emotions that came up every time he thought about his sister, it brought the very human aspect of him home to me. I felt like I already knew him, whereas before, I felt there was such a distance between us just because of his notoriety. He actually moved in an arena where I didn't reside very much, but that moment and story drew me to him. So keep that in mind. It is really important that you create a context in which people can relate to you well.

Be sure to prioritize and post your book cover on all of your online profiles everywhere you can. Some authors put their book cover instead of their own picture on their Facebook pages. We have done that with some of our books in Facebook groups and also in LinkedIn groups. Don't overlook LinkedIn! It is the most powerful social media for business that is available. It is very important that you have a great profile and that you display your "soon to be released" book on LinkedIn. I have many friends who look to LinkedIn as their #1 source for speaking and coaching engagements.

People want to feel they know you on a personal level, so incorporate them in reports on the progress of your book. Include them in your decision-making process. Run chapter titles by them for input. Get feedback on your book cover choices. There are so many decisions to be made during the process of bringing your book into the world. Use social media and blogs to get options and watch how that draws people in because they feel they are a part of the process. They start identifying with you as a person, which will translate into book sales later.

PRESS RELATIONS OVERVIEW

Debbi will now bridge the gap between the publishing side of things and getting hugely promoted because writing is just a small part of the job. Embrace your role as your book's chief spokesperson. If you do that well, you will have a chance to create a long and successful writing career.

DEBBI: I want to stress the importance of a point made earlier about the professional editing of a book. I have been on radio going on ten years. I am syndicated on sixty-five stations. I am doing something right, correct? When I first began airing the show, I had very few listeners and followers, and because of that, I was interviewing lesser known, less influential guests. The point is that you start where you are in any business. You might be surprised at the ways potential guests would try to connect with me in hopes of securing an interview. They'd send me books that had not been edited, with incorrectly spelled words and poor punctuation. You must have your book professionally edited. From a radio station producer's or host's standpoint, you will not be taken seriously as a professional otherwise.

Also important is that you bring your authentic, real self to a radio interview because we can feel how real and relatable an interview guest is. Radio is a medium of sound. We don't generally get to see you; however, we do hear you and we can sense you immediately. We are either captured by your information or story, or possibly bored or repelled by it. In radio, the listener can just change the channel if they are not interested in what's being said, and today, there is a lot of radio program competition out there.

In addition to being on the radio, it is also important to write a book. Your subject matter and who you are that you bring to the show is a package that attracts listeners.

If you have never been on radio, have you wondered what it would be like to be interviewed? What would it be like to build your database and your list from being heard on radio? Have you ever wondered as an author, as an expert, as a coach, as a speaker, what it would be like to field offers from radio stations? In other words, the stations come to you to be the expert on their shows. Have you ever wondered what it would be like to feel relaxed, enjoy being interviewed, have a message, and deliver it with confidence? Have you wondered what it would be like to get booked on a radio show and intimately know what professional packages are needed that you should send ahead of time to the station? What would it be like to increase your book sales because listeners are learning about you and your book and your practice while you are on the radio?

Have you wondered what it would be like to increase the visibility of your name and your books from the "work less—play more" formula, or to hire a team and spend more time doing what you love because these radio interviews are now creating a passive income? That's what being on radio can actually do for you—all of that and more. So let's dive into how to attract radio media to you and how to be radio ready.

All hosts with talk shows on radio or on television need interesting guests to attract listeners or viewers. As an author, you need us, but guess what? We need you, too! We really need great people because it is great people who sell our show. So we want you to be great. Know that we totally support you in having a message that is concise with key points.

When you come on the radio, it is not possible to give us everything in your whole book, why you wrote it, why you love writing, and where you are headed. Understand that an interview is a glimpse into your life. It is like a first date with somebody. You really don't want to know their whole life, right? You are hoping they are not going to tell you everything upfront. By the same token, if you get enough of a glimpse of an author that you are going to read, you may feel like, "Oh, I want to know more about this person."

So on radio, you don't want to ever go on and on to the point where the host asks you a question, and twenty minutes later, you are still answering it. The listeners are going to tune out. Your host is even struggling to stay with you because what they really want is a conversation. It is about rhythm and pace. It is like you are meeting someone at Starbucks and having a conversation. You just go back and forth. The same is true on the radio. You answer the question and you turn it back over to the host so they can ask you another question.

The host may redirect or may go deeper into something you said, so you need to stay kind of fluid. It is absolutely appropriate to sometimes tell a compelling story that will really draw people in, but be mindful of the time. On radio, we have to take breaks. On radio, advertisers sponsor our time. If you are mindful of the format of the show, you can be an amazing guest.

If you want to be professional, you want to present a professional package. Hosts can tell in one second whether or not you have been around the block with media before, and we can tell right away how professional you are based on what you put together and submit to us.

Now, because the packages are a bit detailed, I will go more into that in a future chapter. I will give you all of the insider information, even ideas on how you can make it happen less expensively. Just know for now it is most important that you have a great head shot, a professional bio, and about five talking points in the questions you would like to have the host ask.

I am going to spend one minute here on the bio. It is fascinating to me what I receive and what I see. There are people out there who submit a bio that is poorly written for radio. Then there are people who work with a publicist or PR agent and they have a rocking bio. It is fantastic! It is short enough to be read on the radio, but it literally hits the point with great content.

Your bio should start out with the first sentence stating exactly who you are and what you are doing today. So it might read, "Chuck _____ is a best-selling author and a top expert on money," period. I know right there who you are and what you do. This gets the listeners' attention. The rest is back up information: What is the name of the book? It may be that you spoke on a specific stage that is impressive. Always include notable awards and accolades, any noteworthy degrees or accomplishments, and, of course, your branding URL where we can find you and your work, and where to buy your book. It should be a short but dynamic bio.

This package should be in many places, including the URL you just bought at godaddy.com. Put a little tab on your website that says "Media" because you are going to post your radio interviews there, and you are also going to include all of this information. It makes it so easy for you. Anyone who wants to interview you can go there and download everything. You don't have to keep sending it out over and over.

I also want to cover something really important here, a caveat. So many authors waste a tremendous amount of money. How? They have written this book, it's been published and then they use their own money to purchase copies of their books. Even if it is at wholesale prices, authors are still purchasing their own books and spending postage, which is really expensive, even for media postage rates these days. They are sending it out willy-nilly to all these different radio people and hoping that they are going to get on their shows. Now if you are working with someone savvy like a publicist, someone who really knows the business and is sending books out specifically because you have a strategy and you know why and where you are sending them, that's perfect. That works. That will get our attention.

If you are on your own, you are not aligned with anyone and you are just sending your books out, stop doing it. They are going into a black hole. We do not have time to read them. As a known radio host, I am receiving from Hay House, Simon and Schuster. I am receiving from Penguin. I am on all major publishers' lists to receive their clients' books. I am also fielding all these people who are scheduling on my show months and months in advance. When I am going to interview an author, they send me their book and it is my responsibility to read it. I know that not all radio personalities read the books. I hear it all the time, but what I can tell you is that I do, and it takes time for me to prepare for the guest. I can't read someone's book who is not even booked on my radio show. After you are booked, after you are scheduled, then yes, you will send us everything, but until then, do not bother. That is not how to get our attention.

Why would you want to do radio? We are talking about being an author. Perhaps that's where you are coming from. Why radio? Because it is free press, because we are introducing you to a vast audience who might not have known your work if you never had been interviewed on the radio. Why else? Because when you go on a show that is high level, your interview will be archived after it airs live. Your audio will be available possibly on iTunes, RSS Feeds, and on Podcast sites. Your interview is out there on the Internet, accessible for evermore. Amen. Additionally, it is smart to post the audio of your interview, or a link to it, on your website. You have just become exponential in a big way.

When you master radio, you attract more media, more clients, more book sales, and more speaking gigs. Online radio is everywhere, so you can easily learn interview skills. Start to get booked on Internet radio shows and build your interview skills to have a very clear and easy message.

We live in a mediacentric world. A strong message, a killer pitch, and a winning strategy propel your bottom line.

Media is everywhere. We are our own broadcasters, 24/7. When you learn how to do this right, well, and easily, then potentially everyone becomes your next client, your next customer, or your next fan. As an author, you need to confidently say, "This is who I am, this is what I do, this is what I wrote." That's how you get interviewed on radio.

I am going to tell you a story about John Gray, who has written many books. Most notably he is the author of the book *Men Are from Mars, Women Are from Venus*. After John Gray wrote the book, he did interviews, but he did not earn a penny for a year from *Men Are from Mars, Women Are from Venus*. He was drowning, and was having a tough time supporting himself and his family. What was going wrong with his interviews that were failing to attract buyers, clients, followers, purchasers? John Gray was even interviewed on Oprah. Oprah! *I know, right?!* And even after his Oprah interview, not a darn thing shifted or happened. Why? John was bad at interviews—so bad at interviews that he went back to the drawing board. He knew the one thing in common with being interviewed and not getting results was him.

John got a coach and then learned how to be interviewed properly, how to deliver his message, and how to clearly state his book's message. The rest is history because today, John Gray, the author of the best-selling book, *Men Are from Mars, Women Are from Venus*, has sold over thirty million copies and was on the *New York Times Bestseller List* for seven years. Being the smart man that he is, after being coached on how to properly be a guest and be interviewed, he circled back to Oprah's team, and asked to come back on the show for another chance. She did give him that do-over, and he showed that he had learned how to be "interview savvy." His books sold very well the second time around, and he quickly became known as an expert in relationships!

It's a tremendous thing and very rare for any book to be a *New York Times* bestseller for seven years. Gray's is a great story because that's what understanding how to do a great radio interview can do for you, too.

After I published my first book I had the experience of stepping away from the interviewing side of the microphone as host and moving to the guest side of the radio world. Suddenly, I became known as the success and media expert. I had to learn everything you are learning now and implement it out in the world. I had to learn the skill of being interviewed.

Being a host on radio or TV requires a completely different set of skills than knowing how to artfully be interviewed for results. When you're on the other side of the microphone or camera, you need a different set of skills.

What I have learned about being interviewed and have seen with my clients, is once you do it well and replicate one good interview after another, you start to become known as an expert in your field, and doors open to webinars, teleseminars, speaking on stage, morning drive time radio shows, magazines, Internet radio podcasts. Giving a good interview will open doors for you and your business in ways you cannot anticipate.

As the founder of MediaMasteryRadio.com, I have successfully prepared hundreds of media spokespersons. My clients have included professionals, international speakers, best-selling authors, entrepreneurs, CEOs, business people, transformational leaders, and financial gurus.

A veteran broadcast personality, I have more than ten years of experience in American radio as well as a three-decade-long entertainment career, and I bring this first-hand media experience to every training session. Working with people worldwide, I can assure you, introverts are as terrific at interviews as are extroverts. A beginner can learn quickly, and someone who has already been interviewed, but knows there is something off in their delivery, or is not getting the results they deserve, can always incorporate mentorship in media training and become excellent.

Investment in radio and book programs uplevels your business and message. Learn how to be a best-selling author, how to get booked on radio, and how to get big results. The reason why your business offerings and media appearances don't sell out is because your messaging is off. I can help you sell out and have a waiting list by using media properly when I show you how to message yourself correctly. Learn PR and Media for a successful business. It must be part of your overall business strategy.

DID YOU KNOW...? Oprah Winfrey, Bob Costas, Vin Scully, Al Michaels, and Warren Buffet all had radio mentors and coaches who played a pivotal role in their success?

How about you? Are you ready for a breakthrough to the next level, ready to gain exposure, and ready to change up your game? Are you really ready to get help and acquire some free messaging and PR knowledge? We each come with our gifts, our message, and our unique story. As Viki wrote earlier, when you are ready to get your story out there and really do this, we are ready to help you.

Discover More:
Become a Best-Selling Author and Radio PR Magnet
with Debbi and Viki in a comprehensive class:
BookRadio.Expert

Chapter Two
Your Book
Pave a Smooth Journey for Your Book

Welcome once again to the journey of creating a bestseller out of your book and discovering the amazing ways you can be booked on radio and be relaxed and exquisite while you are on air.

We are really honored to share our experiences with you, and I want to say "Bully to you," for reading this book. ("Bully" is actually a very English term that means congratulations.) The reason why I say, *"Congratulations, a very hearty congratulations!"* is because the excitement of having readers—people who are interested in learning and being coached and mentored at this level—tells me you are really ready to play a big game out in the world.

You are prepared to do what you say you are going to do. I adore people like you because I like creating dreams and turning them into reality. So congratulations to you for aligning with us to learn about being a magnet for PR and media. We are both excited to be able to help you get where you want to be.

This chapter is an overview. I, Debbi, am giving you the flavor of what all this entails. What follows is a bird's eye view of the arc of a book campaign from the beginning to the end.

In the next chapter, Viki will expound on detailed information. Now you have a complete overview, and later we will deep dive into some specifics. You will have all the elements required for a successful book launch.

The flow of how the book operation works is, first, write a book. Next, have a book campaign to launch on a particular day with the intention of creating a best-selling book.

I am not referring to a *New York Times* bestseller; that's a totally different subject. For a NYT bestseller launch, an author can hire an expensive team to handle it. That is what we recommend if you desire to go that route, so you are ensured success. It is a pricey prospect.

What we are talking about in this book is an Amazon bestseller list. To achieve that specifically, you will drive up sales on one day.

So you write your book. You have a fabulous cover, title, and endorsements; the book is properly laid out, and professionally edited. It is all done. Then you launch your book on a particular date. Once your book is launched and out there, or just previous to your launch, you can start booking radio shows.

Once you begin scheduling radio show interviews, your radio appearances will help you sell your books, help you promote your books, help you get the information that your book exists out to a large number of people because people are listening to the shows that you might never have connected with otherwise. Connecting with new, large audiences of listeners is a great PR opportunity, a terrific way to build up your business and ride that wave of introduction to your work, your book and your message.

If you write a book but do no PR or interviews after it is published, you miss out on an incredible opportunity.

PR creates an opening; a viral response. You can ride that new positive awareness of you and your book into different places and venues to experience success in areas you wouldn't have otherwise. PR done properly gives your book a tremendous life after launch, which has a fantastic return on investment.

How do you create a successful book launch campaign? **The first and most important thing is to have a timeline** so that you can execute to-dos in a timely manner. You may be deciding to do the book launch on your own, and it is a robust job. If doing a bestseller launch on your own or with your own business team, give yourself a minimum of six months after your book is written. Six months to one year affords the grace to handle all of the aspects involved in creating a bestseller.

You can also set up a timeline and then hire someone to take care of all the details. You can be the author and let them do the rest of the busy work. Either way, the first noteworthy item to handle is the timeline.

The timeline is basically a map with bullet points, which is much like a calendar. You may choose to do this yourself, or you may have a team. If you don't have a team, you may want to hire one. Similarly, you may want to hire a virtual assistant if you don't have one. You may also want to hire someone who works well in advertising and marketing or someone who is great on the web and social media. All of these team components will work terrifically.

The timeline calendar is not rocket science. There are definite guidelines on what must be handled within those six months to one year, and then there are optional suggestions. Timelines will be covered in depth later in this book. Rest assured, we have your best interest in mind, and this information is being laid out gently so you, our dear reader, can absorb the material and the book process in an easy way.

Regarding any optional suggestions, it is about what appeals to you. For instance, if you wanted to create a book video trailer to introduce us to your book and its message, that can add very compelling benefits about why someone will want to read the book.

I never recommend trying to sell or be salesy; rather, draw people in so that they want to hear more about the book. As always, content is king. Give away information people do not generally know. This way, they lean in to learn more about you and move forward to purchase and read your book.

When you set up a timeline, it is your bestseller to-do list that maps out what needs to get done and when in order for the launch to be a success. There are certain things you must execute, and then certain things you can choose to do or not to do. With any optional promotion, if it isn't fun, don't do it!

For each day leading up to your book launch, the timeline will inform you exactly what items you are going to take action on. Again, I will go into more detail about the timeline for more clarity. I am just giving you an overview right now.

The next piece that is really important for a successful campaign is to **have campaign partners**. Who are campaign partners? They are friends, family and especially influential others who will talk about your campaign. Now some of them may say, *"Oh my goodness! My really good friend Viki just wrote this amazing book. I am so excited because she is one of the most prolific authors I have ever read. You can check out her book at _____."* (If they are posting on social media, they would include a direct link to her book where people can check it out and hopefully buy it.)

When colleagues or friends agree to be our book campaign partners, we do all the work—they just copy and paste the materials we send. **The responsibility we have as an author is for us to write copy or hire this job out.** I have written my own copy forever, and you actually start getting good at it. You may desire to include book tweets you've written; five to ten tweets is a good amount.

Remember: tweets are one hundred forty characters or less; however, a tweet is better if it is close to a hundred characters. Why? Because you want to include your handle. For instance, my Twitter handle is @debbidachinger. For my book launch, I would write a tweet about the book, make it content rich, have the book URL where it is sold, include my handle, @debbidachinger, and also include some hash tags like #love, #fashion, #fitness, and #repost.

I recommend that you create ten tweets and write a Facebook post. Again, content is why people read what we post. Don't just write, "I wrote a book, buy it." No one cares. There are a million books out there. Drive someone's eyes and ears to your social media because it is content heavy. They will learn something and will be moved to know more. Where does special media work for you? Choose those, too, and write copy for LinkedIn, Google Plus, Instagram, etc. That lets the world know about your book in a fun, entertaining or educational way. Additionally, you can write a longer, content rich newsletter and news blurb or blog copy.

The copy you have just written up for your campaign is going to begin with "I" statements because you will be sending all of this out. However, you also want to replicate this same copy in another document and save it because you are going to change the verbiage so that a person (campaign partner) sending it out on your behalf, your influential colleague, will instead have copy that does not have "I" in it; rather, it will read like, *"My good friend Debbi..."* so it is clear your partners are referring to you, the author, and you have done all the work to make it easy for them to copy and send out on your behalf.

To get influential campaign partners on board for your book, consider who you know. Who do you know that has a big database of people—a big following? Who do you know that reaches a lot of people, or has listeners and an audience, or is doing well in business? It is awesome if you include different types of businesses, by the way, because you are reaching new audiences over and over again. Even if it is loving friends who maybe just have one hundred to five hundred people on their lists, hey, that's effective as some of those one hundred to five hundred people may be willing to take action on your friend's recommendation for your book. You are a winner, and you're now selling books.

Now you are also going to instruct people on the exact date to send everything out—that's so important. Why? Well, for example, let's say your campaign date is September 12th, but you start sending out copy and everybody starts sending out copy. What's happening is people are buying up your books willy-nilly any day, and you just lost your launch day. You want to drive sales on one day, so how do you do that?

First, you send out an email. Please blind copy them using "bcc" so that they don't all see each other's names. Using your web mail system, the message can be addressed to them individually: Hi Debbi, Hi Viki, Hi AUTHOR, Hi Bob, etc. Have a very short, to the point email. Remember, you want to do everything above the top line where everyone is going to read before they click off. What is the book? What is the event? What are you are asking them for? What is the date? If they can do this, they should let you know so you can include them. Then it is your responsibility to remind them before the day arrives. Send a reminder for them to put this on their calendars, and provide the copy. Do the same thing the day before and the day of the launch.

The day of our book launch, we wake up very, very early in the morning at God o'clock when it's still dark, and we are up until the bitter end. It is a book campaign, so we are up twenty-four hours watching the book ranking numbers to see when we hit bestseller. When you wake up on your campaign day, send reminders to everybody who committed to help you, and include again the copy of the tweets, the Facebook copy, the LinkedIn copy, the email copy, etc.

You also want to use book forums and social media to create a successful campaign. Book forums are sites like Goodreads, AuthorsDen and your book should, of course, be on Amazon and Amazon's Authors Central. AuthorsDen is a whole description about you, and you can start to write to people, back and forth who are interested in you and your book. Keep things posted there—your events, your book signings, etc.

Social media is your friend, so use social media as well as book chat rooms. Something I highly recommend is identifying who the popular book bloggers are. Book bloggers are our buddies. We connect to the book bloggers. Now they are not very easy to align with because everybody has a book and everyone is trying to get their attention: Interview me, read my book, view my book, have a conversation with me, and let's blog about it! Sometimes ten thousand, one hundred thousand, or even five hundred thousand people are following them. Who are the people following them? Readers, and that's our audience.

So book bloggers can be your best friends. You want to start reaching out and letting them know about you and your book a bit early on your timeline. Each one will ask for different things from you or from your team. Just make sure you get them what they want and need so that you can book some book blogs. This would be tremendous for you. This is all free advertising we are talking about.

So we have created a timeline. Now I just want to pause here to mention something that's really important. I am going to ask you to just relax.

I am a voracious reader. I love, *love* reading. I actually have a leather chair in my living room which is what I always wanted, a barcalounger. I wanted a chair, a lamp and a little table next to it. Why? So I have a space to read where I can just kick back. It's like my little world that I go into with my book. If I am a voracious reader, that means I buy a lot of books. I am going to assume that most of you read, at least, and that maybe some of you are somewhere along this spectrum also of loving the world of books and what they give to us: The rich imagination and places and people they introduce us to that we would never know otherwise.

Why do you pick the book you are going to read? What about a book causes you to read it? Where do you buy your books? Do you go to a bookstore and physically look at books? Do you go online and look at books on your computer? Do you go on your Kindle or Fox Fire or Nook or other electronic devices? How do you choose a book and what makes you buy the book? Is it the cover? Is it the title? Is it that you read the synopsis? Is it that it says bestseller on top? Is it that you know the author and love everything he or she has written in the past?

The reason why I ask you these really important questions is this is what your book is up against. You want to sell your book and what's beautiful is that for each person, you may have a different answer. Some may say that they look at the cover and if it is appealing they may be in. Some may say that the synopsis is everything. If it doesn't have a story line or a self-help subject, they know they won't read it. But if it does, boy, they buy them in bulk. Some may say that they need a title that calls to them; others may say they read the reviews and the testimonies. No matter what it is for each person, understand that each of these components creates an audience, and sometimes it is an amalgam of all these factors put together that compels the reader to buy your book.

I bring this up because you want to look at each of these areas when you are creating your book. You want to know that your title speaks to what's in the book. Sometimes people try to get so clever with titles, which can be fantastic if it still speaks to what's in your book. For example, Tina Faye is a comedian from *Saturday Night Live* and is now an actress and the host of all these awards ceremonies. She wrote this book called *Bossy Pants*. Well, we look at the name and, of course, her name speaks loudly. People are going to buy her book because it is Tina Faye and *Bossy Pants* is something that is very funny that she would say, and that speaks to what's going on in her book.

She can get away with that. For most of us who do not have a president's name or a celebrity's name, we must be very clear to communicate what the book is all about. As a general rule, you have to say it in three words—four if you must, however three is best. To get your title exactly right, you must play, play with words. Oh my goodness, every time I wrote a book, I created pages and pages of titles. Sometimes it is just a process until the best book title floats to the top and becomes clear—that's the title.

I have even run contests and had people vote on a title. For those who say that they can't do that in three words, well they can. We all do.

Then you create your subtitle so that it adds more detail about the book and the benefits. Look for bestsellers on Amazon or wherever you buy books and make that part of your research for good titles and subtitles.

Have a professional, awesome, high resolution photo of yourself for the book. You will be using this for all of your branding, everything you do. You will use it for the cover of your book. You will use it and send it out over and over again, so have a professional photo. I will give you a secret tip. You actually don't have to spend a lot of money. My very first book came at a time when I didn't have much money. I don't remember which discount program I signed up for (it was Groupon or Living Social), but I happened to see an advertisement for a photographer. I researched all of their reviews and everyone thought they were fabulous. I booked this photographer and I also booked my make-up person that way.

If I tell you that I spent under $75 with tips for photos, hair, and makeup, that's the truth. That's the picture you see on my first book, *Dare to Dream*. By the time I wrote my second book, I was doing very well, so I had more money. I hired an amazing photographer and we got tons of photos out of that session. So yes, you must have a good picture, title, subtitle, and bio. You must have a beautiful bio that really speaks to who you are and the amazing things you have done out in the world. Include awards and accolades as well.

You are going to want reviews and testimonies. I say, create a wish list. If someone would read your book and write a testimony or a review that is going inside the cover, or a real big name may go on the outside of the book on the back or maybe right up front. Forget about Oprah! She is probably not going to write a review, but after that I would say it is anyone's game. You could get it now if you write to them or their agent. I am going to bank on those yeses.

Also, you may have influential people in your life already who can write these for you. Send them a PDF of a couple chapters of your book, sometimes your whole book, and ask that they send a review back to you. Give them a deadline by which you want it back.

What else do you need? Well, you need a great cover. You need a fabulous cover for your book. That means the use of color. It is a bit like Feng Shui. Feng Shui is the balance of all the elements in one space. It could be your work place; it could be any kind of business or home. It creates a balance. It creates real ease. It creates cohesiveness. The specifics of Feng Shui are that it connects to the person who resides in that space whether it is work or home, and so it is with your book.

The contents need to also be reflected on the outside. So let's say you really have this somber book going on. You may not want to choose a bright yellow outside with roses all over it. It would be incongruent with what is going on in the inside of your book. So you want to make sure that everything has a flow to it, the vibration, the feel and what's being represented should be consistent. Your cover needs to speak to people who are out there looking at a gazillion books. What's going to catch them and make them want to buy yours?

Cover, photo, bio, testimony, title, subtitle and how the cover is designed are very, very important. I also would like to say when you are creating your book, editing is everything. I am the daughter of a professional proof reader. I don't have the brilliance my mother does—Oh my goodness, she is brilliant! She edited both my books, and even after I took them through five full drafts as good as I think I am, she still took it and made major corrections for which I am deeply grateful. She found a couple of words that I missed and my computer spellcheck missed. She also corrected some syntaxes or methodology of how I put together a sentence. She corrected it for proper English while honoring my message and my words, which is what you want out of an editor.

I also want to address editing in more detail from the stand point of having been a successful radio host for eight years now. I have a lot of authors who come on my radio show. In the very beginning, when I was building my show, I took anybody who had just published a book. I was getting brand new people to the business and brand new authors who were self-publishing.

I would read things and think, "You have to be kidding to put this out like this. You missed the period, you misspelled a word, and the sentence is set up completely erroneously." If you want to align yourself with TV shows, radio, bloggers, and your readers, readers who are spending money for your book, it has got to be quality. It's got to be top notch. You have to be proud of what you are putting out there. You have got to take the time to have it properly edited.

So let me get a bit more into timelines for your book and your e-book. **Six to twelve months before you release your book,** you create a website if you don't have one. If you have one, you can set up a tab for your book or create an adjoining website for your book. What does that mean exactly?

You may have a website, but then we set up a special one for our book. Often the domain name will be the name of the book, but it could be the author's name instead. Allow the two websites to connect. This way, people can click to your book if they are on your main website.

Also six to twelve months before release, you want to create an author page or a blog and at least one or more social media accounts. Why would you not do Twitter, Facebook, or LinkedIn? If you want to, go to Pinterest, YouTube, and Instagram, and keep growing from there. Create these accounts because it is just more people you will reach. Once it is set up, you want to be engaging with your audience through your website, your blog, and your social media about your upcoming book. Remember what I said: It is about content, it is not about, "Hey, I wrote this book—buy it" or "Hey, I wrote this book. It is going to come out soon. Yea me!" That is not going to engage us. You have to create engagement. You can even ask questions that get conversations going and allow people to be heard on these media sites or blogs.

Six to twelve months in advance, you also want to determine your strength. What do you want to add that's fun for you that sounds exciting or different? Perhaps you are comfortable doing interviews. Maybe then you want to look at radio shows, television, or videos. Maybe you are comfortable doing book signings. Determine the local or nationwide bookstores at which you might want to do signings that might also have an interest in you. Perhaps you are comfortable being on stage and you really prefer speaking engagements. You want to build upon your strengths by knowing your book and knowing your material, so that when you speak on stage, or do a book signing, or do a radio or television interview, you know your material so well it flows out of you. Being able to talk about your book is crucial for book success.

It is very important six months to a year before your actual launch to also research your target market. The questions to ask yourself are: What websites do readers of books similar to yours visit, and what groups do they belong to on Facebook? Join them. What magazines do they read? This is your target market, your particular niche. This is who you want to sell to, speak to. Do research on book clubs; do research on blogs, research websites, and research book review sites. All of these can potentially feature you and you book. You want to reach out them. Let them know you exist. Send them your photo and book cover, a very tiny synopsis about your book, a bio about you and how much you would like to be in their book club or interviewed on their blog.

So that's the six months to one year timeline. Let's move on from there to the four to six months period, which is **four to six months before your actual book release.** You want to begin building your email list and communicating with your subscribers. Now some of you already have a really delicious list. That's okay. Start building from there. I don't think anybody reading this book would say, "I don't want any more followers, darn it. Those darn followers, why do they keep following me?" No actually they are our friends, because people who love us send things out virally. It happens to me all the time. I post one of my videos from YouTube (one of my radio shows, for example), or I post something about my book, and there are so many beautiful people out there who will take what I did and send it out without me even asking them. That's a great campaign partner. They believe so much in your work, they are getting so much of what you send, so build your email list and communicate. Remember to focus on content—give your subscribers content.

Four to six months before your book release, you should contact relevant book clubs. Provide copies of your book for review, should they be interested. These are presale copies. Determine when your book will be published and update your marketing calendar. You can also add this to the website you created and in the various blogs. "Books being reviewed by _____, really excited for this date!" You are building up excitement in people for this date to watch your progress. This is what I know for sure: Everyone loves to watch someone's dream come true.

So when you involve people at this level, it's actually an honor for them to watch and witness someone executing their dream, really signing up for this and doing it. When you share it every step of the way, people get excited, and again, this is another opportunity. They start sending things out on your behalf, like, "Oh my goodness, my friend Debbi is doing _____, her book is being reviewed and I am watching when her amazing book is coming out." This person just sent this out to whole slew of people who wouldn't have known about me otherwise.

What else you can do four to six months before your release? Research any upcoming book festivals or events relevant to your book's topic. If there are book festivals, if there are book events, find out how you can get involved. That means maybe you can purchase a vending table or maybe you could be a featured speaker.

Next you can create a media list that would include potential radio and TV outlets, magazines and newspapers that would feature you and your book. Reach out to them. Create your book's press release and media kit. If you don't have one yet, please set up a Google Alert for your name. You are going to use these Google Alerts to add positive press to your media kit. I have Google Alerts for my name, my business name and for a particular subject I am interested in. To do this, you go to Google, find Google Alert and, of course, it is Google so it is super easy. It actually asks you what key words you want to look for and then anything that comes out on the Internet will be sent to you.

For instance, I created a Google Alert for my name, Debbi Dachinger, and I chose "send it to me daily." I will receive a notice when anything pops up anywhere on the web each day. I am amazed where my stuff ends up, in what country, in what magazines that I didn't even know about. It's terrific! You can do that for yourself, for your book, and for anything that is essential for this book launch campaign.

Four to six months before your release, map out a promotional schedule for blogs you can write. You can contribute to a blog that will speak to a subject of interest to the blogging audience. It is actually a blog of content and you can mention your book. You can also do promotional schedules for schools or businesses you can visit, and conferences you can attend that will further help you market your book.

You are definitely going to need a marketing calendar that includes the day to day accounting of when and where your book will be featured. Websites, radio interviews, contests giveaways; if it is on your website, people click on your marketing calendar and see all these amazing places where you are showing up. Again, people see your dream coming true. Some people may even say, "You know, I know somebody who runs a bookstore. Let me write to them about you. Someone else may say, "I have a radio show. Why don't you come on?" It just creates opportunities, and you don't have to do the work for it to happen. It just comes to you.

Four to six months before your release, plan book tours, plan events, and plan book signings. When I say book signings, it means both physical book signings and also virtual book signings.

Now we are down to one to three months before the release. Contact TV, newspaper, and radio contacts from your media list. What do you do for TV, newspaper, and radio? You send them a media kit. You send review copies of your book to interested media.

Now, once they express interest in you, they may say, "I would like further information" or "Great, let's book you." That's when you send out your book, once you get booked on a specific date. You don't send out your book before then. Trust me, doing so will not book you on anything, nor will it create interest. There is one difference. Often, with TV interviews, they do want a pre-copy of the book. However, that is usually handled through different hands, so just trust the process about sending yourself out.

You are going to determine when your book is going to be featured on radio, on TV, and in magazines, and then you add that to your marketing calendar.

You should contact the owners of blogs and websites that are going to feature your book. You will send them press release kits. You ready your books so you can send the review copies once you know from each of these places where and when you are going to be featured. When your book is featured, add it to your marketing calendar. Boy, it is fun to start following where you show up.

Here is a suggestion; it is not a must. You can create a book launch trailer. This is a short video you can create for yourself that's similar to a movie trailer. Remember, people's attention spans are not that long—one to three minutes is plenty.

If you choose to do a book launch event party (this is also a suggestion), you will need to decide on a location, the date and time, who you are going to invite, and what you want to have there. Maybe you are going to have little promotional giveaways. Maybe you are going to sign books. Maybe you going to have bookmarks or a banner made, or balloons, or food. Think about all the aspects of your book launch event party, if you choose to have one.

Now, elevate your pitch. An elevator pitch means if you are going from the first to the tenth floor and someone says, "So tell me about the book you just wrote." You have the amount of time it takes to get from the first to the tenth floor to create compelling intrigue. So what will you say about your book?

When I did my book launch, I was interviewed all over the place, including a lot of main stream radio and a lot of talk radio in the USA and other countries. Talk radio is boom-boom. That means I say something, the host says something, I say something, the host says something—very quick, in and out. It doesn't mean occasionally you can't tell a bit of a story, but it is a format that is very tight so they can move on to the next guest. I need that "elevator pitch" when they say, "Debbi, you just wrote *Wisdom to Success: The Five Secrets to Accomplish All Your Dreams*. Tell me about it. Why are people interested in it? How did you create an international bestseller?" I have ten seconds and *boom*! I have got to get a good response out to answer well and to create intrigue so the host can move on to another question.

Now we are at the book release time. Drum roll, please! You will want to update your social media account and your website revealing when your book is being released, and a link where the book can be purchased. Remember, timing is everything. You want to drive people only on the day of the launch. Yes, send out lots of media ahead of time, but don't sell your book ahead of time because a bestseller is created from one day of driving up sales. At some time during the day of your launch, you will reach a peak. For instance, if your book is on Amazon, you will be watching your book rankings. You will see the picture of your book and you will be able to literally watch as you refresh it where your book is at in the rankings.

Now I am going to tell you that Amazon only refreshes every hour, so it is a little frustrating for those of us who want to follow our book every three seconds so we can see where our book is at. The bottom line is, if your book gets into the top one hundred in any category, you have just become a bestseller. I say go for both top one hundred and try to hit #1. That's really what we all want, to get to #1. You will want to take screen shots as Amazon does not retain bestseller stats. You will want to take pictures of yourself hitting number one, pictures of yourself next to other authors. I can tell you what it felt like for me seeing my book ranked higher than Sir Richard Branson. It was Richard Branson. It was Lisa Nichols. It was Don Miguel Ruiz. So you get the idea. I was ahead of some pretty heavy duty transformational people, and to see my name and my book going number one was awesome! That's what you want.

Now if you are going international like I did with my second book, you can have different tabs open on the day of the launch to see what's going on in Canada, or Japan, or the UK. Make sure you and your team are monitoring when you hit #1. That's celebratory. You've done it. You have done it!

For some of us, many of us, we may hit #1 and stay there for days, weeks or months. Anything is possible, depending on what you do leading up to the day of your launch and the after launch life of your book.

On the day of your book launch, you may want to send out a newsletter announcing your book release to your audience with the purchase URL. Here is another suggestion: You can run contests on various sites, including your own, giving away copies of your book. If you do this, ask those entering to take a picture of themselves with your book or they can even submit what your book means to them on social media with your hashtag. If you require one or both of these things, people are promoting your book launch for you by entering this contest. They are getting a book. Guess who is the real winner here? Yes, they are getting a beautiful copy of the amazing book that you created, but what are you getting? You may get a hundred, a thousand, ten thousand followers. Who knows how many people want to be part of this contest, by letting everybody know about your book for you.

Also, on the day of the book release, continue to use Google Alerts. Remember, you set yourself up on Google Alerts and then you can add any press that comes out about you to your media kit.

You want to also continue to engage with your audience throughout the day. Encourage them to go to Amazon and leave a book review. I love the book reviews I got on Amazon, Goodreads, Authors Central and all these different sites. It is very important because remember the question at the beginning about why do you buy a book? There are many people who read book reviews and see five stars, which indicates to them that this is must read. Good reviews will encourage people to buy your book. Be sure to encourage people to share details of your book with friends. Be active on social media. Make sure to thank anyone and everyone who supported you. Give a lot of sugar and love because a lot of people show up for us and they are doing it because they care. They are doing it because it is exciting. They believe in us. Give them a lot of love to show your appreciation.

So what do you need to gather ahead of time? I think you need to have consciousness going into all this and say, "I can have what I desire, what I desire is to create a bestseller. I am worth it. My book is worth it. I value myself, my time, what it took for me to write this and I value that in putting it out in the world in essence I am giving a gift to the world because I have a unique point of view that nobody would have otherwise."

Also, you need to locate your partners ahead of time. These are people you already have a relationship with and know well. Partners can also be other authors, editors, blogger website owners, people with large databases, mastermind groups, and people who have a large presence on social and professional media. Just know that having a relationship is really essential because if you just reach out, it will not be effective. I have had people do that to me. I cannot tell you how many times people reach out to me on LinkedIn and Facebook. I don't know them from Adam. I never met them. They say, "By the way, I have a book coming out. Would you let your whole audience know about me?" The answer is always no, for two reasons. First of all, I am way too busy, and I don't have the bandwidth to do it. Second of all, I already supported a lot of influential people in that particular way who I believe in, which leads me to my third point.

How can I believe in you? How can I possible tell people to buy something from you? I don't know who you are. I would never do that to my audience. I would only speak about someone whose work I know really should be read. So it's really important have relationships. If you don't have them, start creating relationships now.

You could also align yourself with people and cross promote their book if they cross promote you. You want to get names and emails from everybody who can assist you in your book launch. Again you are going to create a timeline and you are going to give it to whoever agrees to help you. Now further down the line you are going to send out that copy that they are going to use to promote you. That means your copy, your tweets, your email, your JPGs of your book, and so forth. So if you want to leverage the people on your email list, do so by serving them first.

Service is so important here. You need to come from a place of willingness to help them first. An example of that might be to ask twelve people for their help. Ask them to please send out a notice to their email list with an offer for your book on Amazon.com to help push you to the top. You are going to make an irresistible offer of a digital products bonus for anybody who purchases the book on Amazon for one particular day. So in your world, I call this leverage. It is the power of love combined with leverage to help others to assist you.

You want to compile great bonuses. Your influential partners will often be happy to donate something. That could be an audio, a PDF, or music. They are free for the people buying your book, and it is a win-win. To get their free gift, readers would need to give their names and email addresses when they check in to get the download.

Book categories are very, very important. If you have an e-book on Kindle, you can specify two categories on Kindle Direct Publishing (KDP), and you won't see your book on the day of your launch listed on any category unless it is in the top one hundred of that category. Until that time, all you see is this overall sales rank that changes every hour, and it tends to change just pass the top of the hour.

You just had a big overview. Know that we will be getting into more specifics.

I would like to share a little here about self-publishing. That is what this book is really about. I am going to give you a quote by the woman by the name of Deb Werksman. She talks about how it is in essential to hire a competent, knowledgeable editor with good references and a proven track record. She also says that independent publishing has become an important space full of emerging talent, where a writer's success can lead to a strong relationship with a major publisher. It is no longer an "either or" world, and the dream of traditional publishing doesn't have to go away because an author decides to put their work out on their own first.

There is a reason why the industry has evolved where it is now. So many of us were brought up in a world where if you had a book, you would take your manuscript to a publishing house. You often sent it out to many, and you heard stories about the people who got literally over one hundred rejections before their book was accepted, if it ever was accepted. But the publishing industry has gone the way of many other media sources in our country. Here is some educational information to help you understand how the industry has changed.

I happen to be the sibling of somebody who was nominated for Grammy Awards, and his music is on television all the time. My beloved has won two Grammy Awards for Ray Charles albums, and has worked for some of the biggest names in the business.

The music business died the day Napster and all those music-pirating places came out. Managers didn't pick up on what was happening, that there was a change coming and that change was digital downloads. They didn't pay attention. They thought they were golden and people wouldn't really go for digital. Of course, everyone did. It actually became a reality. So the music industry at this point changed, and has been forever changed for decades.

The same thing, by the way, has happened to radio. Once upon a time you only listened to main stream radio on what they called a dial terrestrial. Then along came Internet radio. The same thing happened. All the station owners and managers said that it would never happen. Who wants to listen to radio on a computer or a phone? That's silly! Well, it wasn't silly. Everyone really wanted the digital download. They loved the content they were given. They loved the difference. They loved the variety. It is here to stay decades and decades later. Radio started to go bankrupt and it has had tremendous problems finding its legs.

Guess what? Something happened to publishing, too. The publishing houses we knew once upon a time entered the digital world. Along came Amazon.com and Barnes & Noble.com. People said that it couldn't be done. Well, it has been done. Digital access to content has affected newspapers, magazines, and the print world in a tremendous way.

So is self-publishing here to stay? Yes. Not only is it here to stay, but it is actually the most viable industry right now. It affords you, the author, a way to inexpensively put out a book. Hopefully it is a terrific book, well edited with great content, but you don't have to wait for anybody in order to publish. You don't have to wait months and months the way you would have had to do a few years ago, even if you had a publisher who loved you.

The stories I hear from people I know are that eighteen months later, or even three years later, the traditional publishers still have their book and it is unpublished. It can be very frustrating. You don't ever have to go through that if you self-publish. You can release your book when you are ready to release your book. You can also handle a campaign and create a bestseller. You can do it all on an incredibly inexpensive budget, and have an amazing product. That's tremendous!

You know the fellow who wrote the book, *Rich Dad Poor Dad*, Robert Kiyosaki? He does a lot of author events. This is a very popular guy. This well-known author speaks everywhere, and is interviewed everywhere. Everyone knows his name. He is a very impressive person.

Well, Robert Kiyosaki does talks and he has said with no apology that the only way he would ever put out a book is through self-publishing, bottom line. So we have all done it, we know the benefits, and that's what we are talking about here.

Let's discuss a little bit about book title so that it starts to create a seed for you about what's possible. The greatest authors struggle at some point with what they call their work of art, their book. There has been a lot of advice on the subject but I want to offer the core of what matters when it comes to a title. The first thing is that the title of your book has to be short so it can fit anywhere, it is easy to type, it is easy to write, it is easy to make into a URL, it is easy to tweet and text, and it is memorable. It must be easy to remember.

The more specific, original and short the title is, the easier it is to remember, the easier it is to write down, and the easier it is to type into Amazon. So a title can be both cryptic and easy to recall. I'll give you an example: *Life of Pi*. Remember that book? It is just three one syllable words and we all know that was a tremendous best-selling book for many years. It became an amazing movie. It could also be a provocative title. To achieve this may mean dividing your audience. If half of that division is interested in your book, it is a win. It is often better to split a crowd than to bore everyone. Another element of a great title is that it is easy to say and can be said quickly. It is easy and fast to say at parties, on TV, and on radio. The fewer number of syllables, the better.

Select a great title that you, the author won't get sick of saying one thousand times. Hopefully you will be interviewed that much, or be blogged about that much, or be interviewed by the media that often. Wherever people want you to talk about your book, you won't get sick of the title. The five thousandth time and five years from now, you want a book title you are excited about each and every time you say it. It is super important that the title matches the soul of the book, and only the people who have read the book can help you with that.

Many novels make the title payoff after you have read the book, and in some ways that makes the title more potent than other types of titles. Then there are organic titles, which are titles pulled from something in the book; a story, a term, a name. Here is an example: *The Perfect Storm*. You might not have known until you read *The Perfect Storm* that it is about something that happens at sea. There is actually a horrible storm that is going to occur and if you are a ship, you don't want to be out there. If you are a person on the ship, you don't want to be in that perfect storm. That is a fantastic title. Just know that the greatest authors have struggled with what to call their books. For instance, F. Scott Fitzgerald wrote *The Great Gatsby*. Are you ready for this? Several other titles were considered, including *Trimalchio in West Egg*. Oh my, *Trimalchio in West Egg* became *The Great Gatsby*. Thank goodness!

Just know that if you are not there yet, it is okay. Keep working on it, keep tinkering on it, and the right one will come to you.

FREQUENTLY ASKED QUESTIONS:

AUTHOR: I am actually in the fourth chapter of my book. I have twelve total that I want to complete. I have the heading and I have the subtitle and the description of each of the chapters. When I begin to write, I am able to write freely, maybe three thousand words per day, but I only have a limited time to put into writing. I have been doing speaking engagements and then working full time. I want to know how I can better utilize the time that I have.

VIKI: I find that what I do to make time for different things in my life that are really important to me is I do meditation in the morning. It clears my mind. So then I sit down and every day I identify and prioritize what is it I need to do. Meditation in the mornings every day really helps me stay calm and become more productive. I make time for it. It is just part of my life, like breathing.

I have interviewed a lot of authors and regardless of if they are really well known the world over or just starting out, everyone talks about different methods for making the best use of their time.

I have talked with people who really construct their time and are very rigid. I have talked with people that are more fluid about how they approach their time. That is a very individual thing for each person, and some days you may not be totally devoted to writing. I talked with one gentleman who is an unbelievable composer of music, and we took his novel to bestseller. It took him three years to write it and his novel is almost five hundred pages. What he shared with me was that some days he would just sit down and write ideas that were not necessarily going into the book but the ideas that came to him creatively would inspire him to get back to his book.

I have always been very driven in business, and when I was younger, I used to think that if I ran into a stumbling block, I needed to drive harder. What I tend to do now when I get stuck is relax. We live half the year in Mexico, and we have a beautiful pool that overlooks the ocean. I take a break, go to the pool, and I listen to meditative music or just anything that inspires me.

I come back and give myself the permission to be stuck for an hour, a day, or however long it takes. Usually by the time I get back from the pool, I am unstuck, but it is the difference between "you need to drive harder" and "you need to write three thousand words a day." If you get to a point where you are stuck and it is not really flowing, think about taking a break. Allow your creative force to enter in and really make a difference for you. This has made all the difference in the world for me and my business. I can't begin to tell you how my business just changed almost overnight, and it continues to change and grow because I apply that principle as opposed to the drive, drive, drive theory.

DEBBI: That was an unexpected, amazing answer. Yet another person who talks about the benefit of meditation. It is time to start to pay attention.

I want to add to the beautiful answer Viki just shared with us. I was very much into my first book and juggling an awful lot. What I found was I was super creative with my time and I found ways to write that worked for me.

Frankly, that has been my entire life. I find that I don't do anything the way anyone else does. Some people tend to have limits and say that you can only do something this way, "You have to sit every day for thirty minutes and write, and if you don't do that, you are not going to create." Everything I have ever created successfully has been my way, my rhythm, and I have always honored that unique rhythm.

For instance, when I was doing my first book, I was travelling, sometimes travelling to speak. I would bring my laptop along and I would write in the airport. I would write on the airplane. I got so many amazing chapters done. I did editing, set up contests while I was away at workshops. I did a lot of interesting things at interesting times. Sometimes I was in a vanpool or shuttle going somewhere and I would use that time to write because if you are in a word document you don't need the Internet.

We may not all have the beautiful home and pool and view that Viki was talking about. That's possible for us all, but wherever you are right now, you can work with that. That is your process. If it is a little longer than someone else's, you may not get your book as fast as you would have thought.

Sometimes I can't remove myself and go listen to something peaceful and beautiful. I can't disengage from my book; it needs my attention. Whenever I have been able to do that, I find I get ten times more done. It is like this perverse, fabulous, universal gift that says, "If you would do this, if you would trust me and have faith and do this, I promise you it will be handled and handled easier and better than you could have imagined." I recommend you do that, and, of course, it will help you tap into the words and the message that is going to come out through you for your book. So, honor where you are. Honor the fact that you are currently busy and then find those creative times when you can write.

We are so excited that we are all committed to this journey and together we will get your message out to the world.

Discover More:
Become a Best-Selling Author and Radio PR Magnet
with Debbi and Viki in a comprehensive class:
BookRadio.Expert

Chapter Three
Your Book Promotion
Elevate Huge Book Promotion Success

VIKI: It's time to sit back and enjoy reading what comes next, because we are sharing phenomenal information about books, with the formula for creating really great promotion around books, and also the technical tools that you need to know for making the best decisions on when to publish your book and the direction you take.

In the last chapter, Debbi shared great information as she touched on essentials; I now will go into further detail on that information. One of the things I want to emphasize is when you write a book, the book changes every moment. It is unique, and books are not like any other media. Many people try to write books; however, only a few succeed. I mention it because as authors who have written books, are ready to or have already published a book, you are in an elite and wonderful crowd when you can say that you have authored a book.

YOUR UNIQUE POSITION AND STORY

Throughout the entire world, an author is part of a small group of people, compared to the world population, and you made that happen, which is a wonderful thing. Your book enables you to spread your message and broaden your horizon beyond your wildest dreams. I have never seen anything else in the media that works like a book. I also believe very strongly that not only does it do a lot for you, but it really is your responsibility to get your story out there because no one else can tell your story for you. If you don't tell your story, it will leave a place in the world that's empty that was meant for your story. I really encourage everyone to get their story out in a book.

It is important to know that the book is the beginning of the groundwork on which you lay your life's platform for success, your whole business. So think of it not as a final work, but more of your conversation starter with those who are following you, with those who have yet to meet you, and with many people throughout the world (truly your word will spread globally in our electronic age when you write a book). A book is the most widely accepted credential and received by the largest number of venues. If you find you are attracted to TV and radio, that's terrific. We are going to be covering a lot of information about radio in the next chapters of this book. We are covering essential media for authors: books, PR and radio.

As an author, you may be invited to speaking engagements, to get involved in creating web pages, to write for news print media, and more. Most importantly, you will find yourself engrained in people's minds, and your book is incredibly important for your business and your dream. There are opportunities that lie ahead of you as a published author, so make your book a realization of your dreams and think of ways to send your message out to your chosen audience; it is really important.

Your book requires certain things in order to attract an audience and also to have them purchase it. They need to know the book is worthwhile and they will like reading it. It should engage them and there should be some kind of call to action, even in a novel, really, there is some underlying call to action that makes people think maybe there is a possibility for potential change in their lives. It is powerful, the way they can prosper from actually reading what you wrote. A lot of it you may never see. You may never know who you have impacted; however, it is exciting to have that kind of true impact with people in your neighborhood who know you and with people across the entire globe who don't know you yet, which is important especially if you are writing your first book.

Especially now with the Internet, people are so busy they want concise information; they like pointed information, so position your book to solve a specific problem or to tell a specific story. Your book will be perceived as more valuable to readers if it is specific. There are some medical books and other very tight, narrow venues in which some authors specialize. If you look at the pricing on those books, they are always double and triple other more general books.

Whatever you've written may be the first of many books you may write over the course of your lifetime. Once you get published and you have your book out in the market place, it is not the end of your journey; it is just a start for you to begin to build a platform on which your business will develop and grow. Your book and platform will build your brand, your name, and your expertise. It is a perfect tool to breathe life into all that you do and create yourself as an expert in whatever niche is your specialization. So what does a book require in order to be well-received?

First of all, you need to have tight content. Most people tend to go very wide, especially with their first book and you don't want to do that. You might be packing so much information into one book, that it actually should be two or three books.

You need to have a catchy title and a subtitle. You need to design the cover to be attractive to readers. The cover should be powerful and draw readers in along with the title and the subtitle. If that's done properly, it can pretty much sell the book.

You also have the back of your book to think about and the back of your book is important geography. **Seek endorsements for your book**, especially from well-known names. You want to put those on the back of the book, and include a little bit about why the book is compelling and why people want to read it and benefits from reading the book. These can be done in short sentences, maybe two sentences about why the book is great, and then your endorsements. You might take an endorsement, even if it is fairly long, and cut that down to one or two sentences that are very powerful.

Take the most powerful piece out of that quote, and put it on the back of your book. You can always put your bio and photo on the back of the book as well if you don't have many endorsements. A lot of people like reading about the author and appreciate not opening up the book to do that. Try to have a celebrity write your book's foreword—that is really desirable, as well as getting experts to endorse your book—it gives you all the more credibility.

Debbi touched beautifully in the last chapter on **the importance of having a really good editor for your book.** Editors specialize in different areas of editing books and have different expertise. Therefore, you might run your book by two or three editors before it finally goes to print.

Evaluate your publishing strategies. Depending on your strategy, you may need an agent or require a publisher; and there is also self-publishing with real benefits. As we mentioned earlier, the world of publishing has changed as a result of the self-publishing option for writers. You will decide whether to get promotional support for your book or do it on your own, or if you need to hire a publicist. If you have joint venture partners, and if you are involved in networks, that will support your book launch. Analyze what that looks like before firming up your plan.

Expect to do all of the marketing for your book, and that is the biggest job. It is important enough to mention again here: Writing the book is five percent; the rest of it is all getting the word out. There are fabulous tools you can use when you act as your book's publicist if you don't have that skill or you don't care to develop that skill to market your work yourself.

When marketing your own book, it is wise to hold high standards for yourself so your book has a good chance of making bestseller and getting unlimited exposure out there in the marketplace. One of the biggest advantages of self-publishing versus a traditional publishing house is that you can inexpensively self-publish, have total control and turn it around in a weekend.

Once again we stress, it is incredible what can be done now through self-publishing. Debbi is a fine example of an author who has certainly had great experience with her books multiple times, becoming #1 international bestseller.

DEBBI: I appreciate hearing these facts from Viki. This is important information as so many authors go out with the excitement of their book thinking, "I have arrived, I have landed," but as writers, we are not educated to the possibility that we *haven't landed* if no one bought our book and no one is reading it, and—sadly—perhaps no one even knows the book exists except its author. In our excitement of having put all the work and time into writing our book, on the back end when it is published, often if the only readers are our circle of friends and family, it is a very small circle.

Instead, what we are talking about is the importance of marketing your book, using your unique point of view and perspective. It is important to find the ways of promotion that works for you and to give yourself a wide berth of time to do so properly.

It takes energy to engage in this kind of campaign and I strongly recommend you write a book if you are 100% in it to win it—and to be in it to win it, you need to be involved in your book's campaign. Give yourself the time to successfully start and complete your book launch. Honestly, it can be tiring for the best of us. When you do the research, you see people who are writing experts, and realize the marketing piece can be a full time job. If you already have a job and you are marketing your completed book on top of your day job, it still can be done, I promise you. It definitely, successfully, can be done and requires appropriating marketing time judiciously done on a daily basis.

A key to that is to plan ahead. If you were planning an event like a wedding, as a member of the wedding, or as the wedding event planner, you would begin six months to one year in advance to plan something really extraordinary. The same thing applies to your book. Your book *is* a wedding of sorts; it is a birth to be celebrated; it is an event. Give yourself a nice amount of time: six months to one year, a little bit more time if you have a job, and know that you can and will run a successful campaign, that you will take care of all the elements, that you need to pay attention to the timeline and launch details. Also, be kind to yourself in the process.

It takes a lot of attention and energy and the book launch journey is incredibly exciting. With each interview you have on the radio, with each review of your book that appears in a newspaper and magazine or a on a blog, with every time somebody reaches out who has read your book, with your book signings and book video trailer, you are going to have the most amazing ride. With every book that you publish, the experience is brand new, so be in it to win it. Give yourself the time to do a book launch campaign successfully. It will be life changing. It will seriously promote your book. You will be positively changed as will your business, and your message will be out where it was meant to be.

VIKI: I agree and thank you so much for your enthusiasm, it is contagious and wonderful. This is a good segue into addressing **the difference between a *New York Times* bestseller, (which is often coupled with traditional publishing), and doing an Amazon bestseller book launch.** Traditional publishing houses also publish on

Amazon, which is a wonderful platform for self-publishing, too. Amazon does not reveal their mechanism or the formula behind their ratings, as it's more complicated than just sales.

With self-publishing, to properly promote a book on Amazon, we cover all the basics: book positioning, sales, visits to the book's Amazon sale page, and lots of five-star reviews from readers. These things may all have an impact.

We do extensive research so that your book is positioned for comparison with similar books on Amazon. They rank their books on an hourly basis, but they don't keep any history on the books, so you want to be either watching the ranking and sales yourself or have someone do it for you by going online to look at the book hourly. On the day of your launch, take screen shots as the ranking climbs to bestseller because that's going to be the only proof you will have that your book achieved bestseller status on Amazon.

DEBBI: *New York Times* does require eight independent book outlets reporting book sales over a one-week period. The outlets can be Amazon book sales as one, a mom and pop bookstore as another, Barnes and Noble as the third, and so on, totaling eight outlets combined together to see if you have achieved best-selling status. Note that it is not easy to achieve, and authors rarely will attempt to accomplish this on their own.

VIKI: The important thing we recommend is that you self-publish unless you have such a burning desire and a life dream to become a *New York Times* bestseller. I have friends who are multiple time *New York Times* best-selling authors, and they have spent copious amounts of money on every book—anywhere from a quarter of a million to half a million dollars to get to *New York Times* best-selling status. This money includes the cost of promotional fees, having to buy and guarantee the placement of their books in bookstores, and distribution with assurance that the author will buy back their books if they are not sold.

DEBBI: The other day I was out with a friend who is a transformational leader, she and I are friends with people whose names you know, who do workshops on self-development. I was just contracted by another transformational leader and company to head up their book campaign; my friend and I were having a discussion about this since she knows them as well. She and I were impressed as this company had just spent a quarter of a million dollars in order for their book to become a *New York Times* Bestseller. She said "I would rather give that money to children that are in need."

These clients spent more than a quarter of a million dollars because they wanted to have a *New York Times* Bestseller. Additionally, besides paying a publisher and an agent, they spent more money when they also bought ten thousand copies of their own books just to bump up records of their book sales, which is a trick some authors use. Many in the publishing business do not appreciate this falsifying of those sales records.

In recent news, a politician was found to have done just this—running a *New York Times* bestseller campaign and buying his own books. He is currently getting a lot of heat in the media while losing constituents, because it was a fake way to run a book campaign and did not gather respect on any front. It's as though the author is saying, "Hey, the public didn't buy my book so to turn my book into a *NYT* bestseller, I will literally buy ten thousand books myself," which is a lot of books. Have you ever tried to store ten thousand books, or warehouse that amount in your home or office? Maybe it is helpful that these particular people are well known, so chances are they will gift these books or sell them at the back of the room at one of their many workshops.

Still, I am just giving you an idea of what goes on, since besides the amount of time to do a *New York Times* bestseller launch and all it takes, it is also really expensive on several fronts and there is no guarantee of success.

VIKI: I interviewed a very famous author a few years back and she was in the middle of a book launch and she was sharing with me how it was the twentieth interview she had done within the book's forty-eight-hour launch period. That was the expectation on the part of her traditional publisher, that she would just knock herself out for forty-eight hours straight while her book was being launched. Listening to her, the schedule was pretty gruesome. It need not be so with self-publishing.

If you want to publish with **a New York traditional publishing house,** you can make this goal of becoming a *New York Times* Bestseller a viable one by getting an agent to help you get your book proposal in the right hands and to help you build offers. It does have an enormous price tag; however, if it is your dream, I don't discourage it. If you are on the fence about it, there is no question: I would go the direction of self-publishing.

At this time, I'll go over **the book proposal** required especially if you are doing a nonfiction book. Book proposals are important for developing a relationship with an agent, so we will go through this quickly so you become a little familiar with it if you are not already aware of how this works for traditional publishing.

If you have a fiction book like a novel, you'll find that they refer to a book proposal more like a query or cover letter and then a synopsis of your book and an outline. You will be sent an email and there may be other information that an editor or an agent requests but it doesn't really have the same meat that a true nonfiction book proposal has.

One of the advantages of a book proposal, if you are going to the more traditional route, is that you can do a proposal before the book is finished and that way you can get an idea of whether or not if it is going to be marketable before you put a lot of work into the book. One of the things that is required in the proposal is the reason for the book to be in existence. This is important for you and a potential agent or publisher.

What is a unique selling proposition, and who is going to care about it and buy that book? What sets it apart from others in the marketplace? You have to define your target readership and just the book being unique is not enough, you really need to also show that there is a marketplace for your work. Next, who are you? You should have sufficient credentials that you have written a book and you have to have an appropriate and dazzling marketing platform and plan for the subject audience. Publishers are going to want to know how many people you have in your database and followers list, which helps with a really good marketing plan.

The editors and agents only care about one thing—if it is a viable idea with a clear market plan paired with a writer with credibility and marketing savvy. If you are not in that position yet, self-publishing is definitely a good way to go.

Additionally, I am going to give you an idea of what a proposal looks like because if you are going the traditional route, you can't go anywhere without a book proposal.

It has a cover page and the proposal table of contents (not the book table of contents, which comes later). Let me give you a little idea of what you are getting into here. It has an overview, maybe a two-page summary of your entire proposal, and it really needs to make a strong business case, so they want to go on and they want to read more. It needs to acknowledge your target market that you have done some extensive research on this, like statistics, and you have facts about why someone will buy the book and why it will sell. A proposal shows that you have done your homework; that you have done a competitive analysis on other book titles and why yours is different and better than other books that are similar to it.

Having a book that no one has written before may not be an advantage as it may be too far out there and they will not want to take a chance on it. But if you mention similar books that are doing well in the marketplace, showing that there is an audience for the content, but yours is different, and point out why it is different or better, that's your best possible scenario. They will expect to see your bio and your platform, to know how you are going to promote your book, and to see a complete marketing and promotional plan for the book. They will not be assisting you on this. You are selling them on the fact that you can sell your book.

Included would be a chapter outline and a table of contents for your book along with sample chapters. That just gives you some idea of what is involved in a traditional publishing book proposal. That's your starting point so, if you are on the fence about which direction to go, this will give you some clarity about how important it is for you to choose because it is great deal more work than self-publishing.

One thing I want to stress is about the power of book anthologies (collaborative books with multiple authors). We have had authors in our book anthologies that have had major media appearances. One of the girls who wrote in one of our women's books landed a prestigious director's job by bringing her book in and talking about it. It was for a company that helps organizations raise money for breast cancer, and she landed this job by bringing in her book and talking about how important women's causes were. She showed she was a best-selling author and she landed the job without even a call back. They hired her on the spot. So an anthology can be that powerful and this one was an Amazon bestseller.

Another advantage with self-publishing is that it has immediacy. When your book is ready and formatted, you can put it up on Amazon and within twenty-four hours that book is going to show up as ready to be purchased. It is like a miracle to me because I have been in advertising and marketing for decades and there was a time when all of this was so hard, doing any research around your book or around its competition or the viability of the book—you had to pay for all of that. Now it is readily available on the web, and it's free! Today you can do it yourself; you can find everything you need including information on your book proposal development on the web.

There are a few places where you can set up yourself to publish a book online. **When you self-publish a book, you have total control of the content, the direction of the book, the timing of bringing the book out, and the royalties.** It's very important that the money all comes to you. If you will write future books, you have the option to do whatever you want with your future books. A number of our authors who have come to us to help them make their books bestsellers have previously been with big publishing houses who take options on their next one or two books, sometimes more than that. So if you want to publish with publishing houses, you may have to promise that they have the first option, with their terms in place, to publish your next book. Maybe you had a bad experience with them and, unfortunately, they have total contractual control for future books. When you self-publish, you have total control over everything, including future books and most important, royalties, which is your income.

We tried all sorts of different things to set up paperback books and the best for us is CreateSpace, which is owned and operated by Amazon. They do a fabulous job of setting up books. We have never had complaints and some of our anthologies have had as many as one hundred authors from across the globe. CreateSpace ships and fulfills orders for you on demand and their ability to get books through customs is incredible. We have gone a number of other routes where that was not the case, so I highly recommend them. As an Amazon company, they have got their act together.

CreateSpace also has templates that you can download to the size of book that you want to put together. You can use a Microsoft Word template for the interior, and they also have cover templates. They tell you exactly what the specifications are so you can put that together, or you can find someone to help you with the technical end of this if this is not your area of expertise; you can find people who do some of this very inexpensively. One of my favorite finds is Fiverr, and there are many potential people to employ there (www.Fiverr.com) who do unique and wonderful things for five dollars and up. You will find talented freelancers who may turn out a really good product for you.

CreateSpace has customizable reports which are great. You can set them up the way you want them to appear, search on how you want your royalties to appear, and if you have multiple books, you can create reports by the book. They directly send you the report so you know how much money you are making and you have direct access to reports anytime you desire to go online and see what is happening with your book's sales.

The royalties come directly to you. When you sign up, they ask you how you want to get the royalty money: if it is by check or deposited into your back account. You give them your preferences online and royalties automatically roll over to you. They also provide you a custom author and book sales web page which gives you a link that shows your book with a picture, your author's biography, and whatever information you put in about your book to encourage people to buy it. You can also activate discount codes to this page.

Also, you don't have to buy any of your own books! You can direct people to your Amazon book sale link and when the book sales happen, you get a decent percentage of the royalties. They do all the fulfillment, and they ship the books to the purchaser, so it is very easy because book buyers can be from all over the world and no matter how remotely people may live, they will receive the books from

CreateSpace. They also have highly discounted wholesale prices on books; CreateSpace.com is print-on-demand. You can order one book or hundreds.

Even if you can only buy one of your own books, you'll still receive a discounted price. For instance, my bestseller book is a hundred-sixty pages and that book is a little over two dollars for me to buy wholesale. My price is so inexpensive to purchase that I can give it away at various organizations. It is less expensive to give away my book than for me to create a brochure because they so reasonably priced.

Kindle is called KDPAmazon.com for creation of your e-book; you can open a Kindle account in about two minutes with an email address and password. KDP approves everything and processes usually in less than twelve hours after set up for sale on Amazon, and many times it is ready within a few hours. Your book is up there and ready for readers to purchase.

They also do fulfillment on Kindle. As people download your book to their Kindle, they access it from their computer or up on the Cloud, and you don't have to have a Kindle e-reader to be able to buy Kindle books. Anyone can buy a Kindle book. They also have customizable records so you can determine what you want to see, how you want to have it delivered, and the record comes to you in Excel format.

The KDP royalties go directly to you, the KDP formatting will accept PDF, however PDF is not ideal. It is preferred to use what they call a Mobi formatting and this can be outsourced if it is something you don't know how to do.

Additionally, for your e-book I recommend that you put some kind of valuable give-away gift on your website in exchange for website visitors' names and email addresses. For instance, if you have an international bestseller, you can suggest someone who visits your website opts in with their name and email address, and in return you will give them a chapter or two out of your best-selling book for download. We also use flip book technology for their ease of viewing. Then you can offer them a purchase opportunity to buy the whole book on the same page. This is just another way that you can promote your book and use it as a desirable gift or partial give away, and also another way to sell it. Just a few ideas.

I will briefly mention Smashwords.com, an e-book distributor to about fifteen major book distributors. They use an ePub format and they are very selective about the formatting as their e-books go out to many distribution sites, like Barnes & Noble and iBook and some really powerful places where readers can find your book for purchase. They also have excellent sales reporting capabilities.

You can see you have a lot of choices and all this is done within your own capability, with the freedom to do anything, any time with any of these resources. It makes self-publishing a really positive, powerful way to go.

DEBBI: I have done everything recommended here, for all of my books, as well as my clients' books and this bestseller campaign is essentially a successful recipe. It's about cooking up an effectual book launch, and for most people cooking with a recipe is extremely helpful to making a delicious dish. Especially if somebody has cooked a fantastic dish and you want to replicate that dish. If you follow how many cups of one ingredient, and how many ounces of another, specifically following their recipe, you will create the results you desire and have a fantastic dish at the end.

It is the same with the book campaign. What Viki and I are sharing throughout this book is a recipe. If you align with these ideas, action steps, recommendations, secrets, and suggestions that we are explaining here in detail, then the end result will almost always be a best-selling book.

The good news is that, with a self-published bestseller campaign, for those of us who enjoy some control and like to know that our efforts are going to be fruitful, we can rest assured that if we follow these recommendations and align ourselves with the amazing information given away in this book, we will enjoy a very successful book experience.

Our recipe offered here is very good as we've experienced the positive outcome for ourselves and our clients. A best-selling book campaign can be fun, too.

POWERFUL CAMPAIGN TIPS

VIKI: On the subject of positive outcomes, I will share tips about a powerful campaign and how to promote it. I have over one hundred and one great ideas and I am not going to go through them all, I am just going to go through a few.

One of the most important things you can do is post your book on websites like Goodreads; also you can go on Google and type "Post for book website," and you will find all sorts of ways to network with other people to get support for your book. There are places available where you can post your book outside of normal distribution centers, which is so powerful.

You can put up a testimonial review page right on your website, and even if you are just building your book, you can give them a chapter to read and ask for feedback. Get them involved in what you are doing. The side benefit of this is that your Google rating will go up through the roof if you have a lot of people contributing and you are answering back to their blog posts on your website. This is a wonderful way for Google to move you up in ratings. We would all love to be number one on a Google search. Therefore, it gives you so much power.

Create a Facebook fan page—it's free. All you have to do is set up a fan page for yourself or your book. We used to do one for every book, but now we have a fan page called BestsellerLaunchPad, where we post everything for all of our books, for all of our authors, and we have over thirty-five thousand followers on that fan page. So when we do post there, it is a very powerful forum and that's just one of our fan pages.

We probably have about ten fan pages on Facebook, we have two groups on LinkedIn, and we have about eight groups we post to on Twitter, with multiple twitter accounts. I am not suggesting that you do that; I am suggesting that you do have a presence on social media, and Facebook and Twitter are fine to start with. I would include LinkedIn and YouTube, as well. It is easy to do videos and send messages to let people know that your videos are available. Make them just one or two minutes, and as I mentioned, tweet, because Twitter is fantastic.

DEBBI: Also sign up for Google auto ship. It is very simple. All you do is Google how to, and you will get full instructions on how auto ship works and what it does. It includes all of your publications, any articles that you write, anything back to you on Google, and essentially this pushes your Google ratings really high.

VIKI: Also, it is important to clean up your social footprint. Be careful what you put on social media. We all know these days that social media lives on forever. There are companies and people out there who will do a search for various reasons. If you're applying for a job is one of them, and finding info on you or anyone is easy! Now regarding who is looking at doing anything with your book, even people like Debbi and me who are radio hosts always Google people who will be on our radio show, and if there is something questionable, it can turn people off. Please know if something questionable exists online about you, there are companies that can help you clean it up and you need to take care of it.

So we have covered some unique and wonderful ideas to get some attention drawn to you and one of the ways is through press releases and press kits. Again, it takes money to hire a publicist. It's not cheap. Usually, publicists will charge you five thousand dollars a month. Some charge as much as fifteen thousand or twenty thousand dollars a month, so it's not inexpensive to do this, but if you have the mind-set and that's attractive to have that done for you, it is worth looking into.

I personally think it is more fulfilling and fun to learn how to become irresistible to the press by yourself, and one of the things that is important is to have is a press kit. Debbi touched on this earlier and I am going to go a little bit deeper. You need to have a hard copy and you also need to have a press kit on your website.

I cannot tell you how frustrating it is for me running two magazines, plus two radio shows and many times I have guests coming on who may not send me their media kit in time, so my team has to search many different online places to try and find photos of them, bios and all that is required for media. Some of these people are in positions where it surprises me that they don't have this together in advance. Then again, the majority of professionals does have a media kit and are timely in submitting, and I am impressed by them.

How are you, Debbi, with people who have it together when it comes to press kits?

DEBBI: My feedback when people don't have a media kit properly put together? Today, to be professional and to be seen as a professional, to do the work you want to do, at the level you want to play, you must have a media kit completed and ready to be sent to whomever is going to feature you.

The rare time I experience someone who is "not yet put together" in this area, I am not exactly excited to work with them; lack of professionalism can bode poorly and cause those in media to have to do work that does not belong to us, in order to feature you.

Also noteworthy, what if a producer searches for you online and pulls up what they see and that's what they run with—and what if that information is old, outdated, or faulty? What if it is an old picture that you do not prefer or a website you no longer use? If you want to be represented correctly, it is each of our responsibilities to have a press kit, and update it regularly. This year alone, I got my coaching certificate, as well as received two prestigious awards. So I had my website updated with these accomplishments and my press kit is updated as well, everything now shows this current news.

VIKI: It is extremely important when sending photos to media, to use only a very high resolution picture. I am often surprised at why someone would not have a high resolution photo on their website so if needed, all we have to do is go to their site and download the hi-res picture. If they are pixilated or poor quality photos, we have to dance around it and the effort becomes so laborsome.

It is also important when you are creating relationships with the press or with the media that you have a letter of introduction. In the industry, the introduction is called a pitch letter, which gives people of interest important information about you. If you are pitching your company, it is great to have material about your company and profiles. For instance if you have anyone that's part of your company who is senior management, send bio sheets and let them know about your company and what the company has done. Include recent press publications and articles, which are welcomed by the press.

When I receive a pitch letter from someone who has been featured on TBS, Oprah's network or show, or on *The Today*

Show, those levels of media outlets really peak my interest because they are going to be a great interview. If you have been in publications or articles through other media, be sure to include that. It strengthens your position enormously.

Press releases that are recent should be included, or if you have pictures of articles, that have been done up for you. Pictures of you in magazines or on the covers are positive. I know Debbi uses an email signature with a picture of her on the cover of *PUBLISHED!* Magazine. I was recently voted in by *WE* Magazine as one of their *Women of the Year,* and when I get the cover, you better believe that's going to be everywhere because it is important for credibility.

For your websites, use audio and video files—examples of anything you have done on air and on TV. It doesn't have to be the hour long interview; it can be abbreviated by posting only a short edited clip. If you can show snippets, it will encourage more people to want to have you on their shows.

Sample news stories give them questions that they can ask you. Debbi can probably attest to this as well. When people supply me with questions for an interview, I might not stick to their questions like a script, but I am going to cover at least some of those questions. Debbi, would you say you do that, too?

DEBBI: Good question. I appreciate receiving questions in advance when I am going to interview someone to get to know better what they want me to shine the light on when we have a conversation. Generally, I am going to follow their questions first, and then things will come up in the conversation about which I become curious, and new questions flow from there. I don't want anyone to send me questions *and* the answers. I do not require their notes or the way they are preparing to answer. Just the questions will do. As a radio host, I may change it up for spontaneity and if I want to dive a little deeper into something mentioned, I will, so never be married to the material you send, and know it may be used. Some hosts will rely on your questions more than others. There is one bottom line and that is that you are an expert and you know the material, so you can field just about any question about your subject.

VIKI: Yes, that's true and it may depend on how busy the host is. I just did an interview for a book that is going to be released soon and one of our contributing authors sent questions and she gave me four other questions that she wanted inserted so she can get certain points across. By all means I would do my best to make sure we covered everything that she wanted to express. I think it is important to at least send an opening question ahead of time so they, as well as you, are prepared.

Also, if you have done any community service or non-profit work, it can touch the hearts of those in the media and give them something interesting to talk about if it applies to what you are doing. Additionally, if you have white papers and if you have mission statements and goals and objectives that are attention-grabbing or something that really intrigues the media, something that's topical like it is happening today, that's going to strengthen your positioning with the media—no question about it.

DEBBI: Agreed. Stories are tremendous to offer the media, especially if you have an interesting one that is different. Just a story of note, a woman by the name of Charmaine came on my show and was a pet owner. You might think that most of the people I know have a cat or a dog. But *her* dog is very particular. Her book and story is that when she and her husband acquired this dog, it literally ate and destroyed her entire house. In order to rehabilitate this dog, they went on an amazing journey, and as part of the dog's healing journey, *they* were rehabilitated and their lives completely changed.

The story was so incredible that Charmaine wrote a book about it. She was featured on my show and she brought her dog Toby to the radio station. It was awesome for me because I love animals and thought it was a unique angle to have Toby at the radio station with us. Toby's story is now being made into a movie. So even though this came from a subject where it could have been just a woman and her husband with a dog, it was actually quite different and heartwarming and filled with wisdom—a journey for all three that created an incredible life for the people and Toby the dog.

I also want to share that this person used to have a government job and now she is a sought-after speaker who brilliantly utilizes sponsorship, and is very successful—just from having Toby the dog and her book and story. So what is possible when you put your message or story out there in your unique way? For someone else to tell your story may be passé; however, you can tell it in a way that nobody else will and be very successful.

VIKI: Yes, and although it may seem like a small part of their lives it is big because a pet becomes a part of your family. The authors you are mentioning didn't have to tell their whole life story in that book, just a small segment of their lives together and look at what that writing did for them.

DEBBI: Exactly right.

VIKI: I will cover some **press release tips** as this is important, too. These are releases that you are going to send out to the media. We send these out with every book that we promote. We send them out to radio stations, TV stations, bloggers, and websites. We follow a specific formula to make sure these press releases get read. You may get calls for interviews, but there is usually more follow-up required. If you want to get interviewed, do a press release. A press release can also generate an enormous amount in the way of Google ratings—we do this for all our authors because we think it is important to get their names out there as well as the names of their books.

For a great press release, you need to start with a powerful, timely, hard-hitting headline which means it has got to be topical. You can go way out there. For instance, the publicist that we work with on occasion put out a press release one time with a headline that read: *Pizza is Cure for the Common Cold.*

It sounds outlandish, but that's how he led the media into the press release. The release covered a new pizza company that he was representing that put pineapple on their pizzas. They put extra pineapple, which has pectin in it, and as a result, it was positioned that their pizza was a cold cure because it contained a great antioxidant.

The headline drew people in and they got tons of interviews from that press release. It may sound a little misleading, however, there are so many press releases vying for attention, a good headline has to draw their attention. Right now, if there was a subject that you were an expert on, for example a health expert who could speak to what is happening now around a health epidemic or perhaps an expert who can talk about a political situation that is very timely—the timelier a subject matter is, the more attention it will grab. The subheading is another hook; it gives you a second chance to hook in the interest.

The press release's first paragraph describes what the release is about. It is your who, what, where, and when paragraph. The body of the press release should contain any claims, and it may contain powerful quotes about your book. If a book has quotes, especially from someone well-known or someone with credentials, it is suggested to put at least one quote in the press release to strengthen the author's position. Finally, keep the press release to one page.

The contact information goes down at the bottom of the release which is where you include your email, phone number, or the contact name of whoever will set up your interview if a release press generates an inquiry for you. Also give out a link in the press release where they can preview the book such as Kindle that has a "look inside" capability. CreateSpace also offers the look inside with the paperback version of your book. It is real important that the full release does not exceed one page. Those who read through press releases don't have time to rattle through a lot of pages. Sometimes authors will send us press releases that are four pages long, and we immediately cut them to one page because no one is going to look at four pages of press release.

Another thing, make sure you are available at a convenient time for anyone calling from the media as they usually give you very short notice to be interviewed. Most of the time, they have a spot they need to fill and they may call you in the morning to be ready in two hours or for that afternoon. It does not always happen like that, but it can, and you are building an ongoing relationship with people in the media so you want to accommodate their schedule the best you can. I heard some experts say, *don't ever say "no" to the offer to be interviewed!* Figure out a way to make it happen because if you say "no," they will not forget it and chances are you will not have a second chance.

Now let's talk about how to get your book endorsed. **Endorsements for books** are very powerful. Something I have learned from building relationships with people is that you must find something that you can do for them. Don't go in asking them what they can do for you. Foster the relationship in advance and do something for them. We developed our radio shows and our magazines so that we could showcase people who were really well known, and we do something for them to start building a relationship.

That was the whole purpose of our radio shows and magazine, initially. Now they serve a lot of additional purposes, but that was our initial reason for developing them. So find something that you can do for others of influence, get engaged in their work and in their research, and include their discoveries and their expertise. I have a friend who is a *New York Times* bestseller and she tells me that with every single one of her books, she does research on the work of experts, and she will email or call them and say that she is looking at their research and tells them how much she admires their work. She'll talk to them about their ideas and as a result, builds relationships which become very positive. Many of them are more than happy to write forewords or endorsements for her.

Give others credit in your book. This is also a good idea for people who are doing work for you. A lot of times, you can get discounts or you can get people to do work free for you if you will mention them in your book, such as editing and cover design services, so keep that in mind.

Attend events; be very familiar with the work that others are doing and express your admiration. Debbi is a master at this and I think you will agree, Debbi, that's how relationships are built, with ways you can do things for people, and soon, they will desire to do things for you.

DEBBI: Wow, I am telling you this is a great education when you address little intricacies such as this secret about creating relationships in business—a select few get this and not all know. Establishing and nurturing a quality relationship with others and putting the spotlight on others are tremendous ways to accelerate quickly in the world.

Even if you look at this principle spiritually, it works: *As you give, so shall you receive.* When we offer our time and attention from a sincere, heartfelt place, tenfold and more is given back to us. There are amazing people out there, doing amazing things and we can be in relationships with them. How incredible is that? I have gratitude also being a recipient of the same when I consider the radio shows that have interviewed me, the features on television shows, magazines or those who reviewed my books; to anyone who basically gave me free press and promotion and only asked me to show up and share my own voice. I am really grateful and consider this karmic reciprocity. I do extend myself to others through social media about the press and inform everybody by saying check out this person and the good work they're doing, or listen to our interview. When I do that, some of my followers and database will start following this person too, so yes, cross-promotion is tremendous, as well as shining the light on others.

I also know a branding business woman who has built an entire business by getting away with certain behaviors on social media that I generally considered a no-no, but she makes it work because she creates tremendous fun and engagement. So every time somebody responds to something she posts, she always writes back to them. I don't know how she has the time to respond at that level and keep the flow and conversations going—she keeps writing back to all these people on Facebook, which is not generally a good place to do business since it is a social friend site. All this is to say that rules are meant to be broken. In general, don't do business on Facebook, then again this branding woman writes terrific appealing posts that receive a lot of responses, she then responds to all responses and keeps it going. There is a lot of love for her on Facebook and she generates almost all of her branding clients from Facebook. This behavior is uniquely indigenous to her personality. She can do this because this is who she really is, and so her followers feel her sincerity and get involved. That is very rare. The take away is *not* about Facebook; the take away here is about the power of connection and relationship and what it creates.

When you affiliate and link with others, their business can bloom because of it. Do not underestimate how much relationships can produce. It is a really beautiful way to do business.

Also noteworthy, what comes to you down the road is in divine order. It may not come back as offers or favors directly from the same people you have helped. I have found that sometimes it does come from those I showed up for, and often, kindness has come to me from places and people who offered me their thoughtful help unexpectedly.

VIKI: Exactly. And don't overlook the idea of networking with people who you know. Another thing that we have done with our magazine is that we have connections with significant people to bring us interviews. Debbi is one of our guest columnists who brings us wonderful interviews with famous people. We featured Debbi and Melissa Manchester a few editions ago, and before that, one of our columnists brought us an interview with Marianne Williamson. We have showcased Deepak Chopra and Jack Canfield, and all of these interviews came from wonderful relationships. I didn't originally know these people myself.

For instance, Debbi and I became good friends, and Debbi suggested that we could do a wonderful class together as we have similar backgrounds and very complimentary experiences that we can share with those who take our classes, attend our programs, and read this book. From there, our relationship has blossomed in a relatively short time to a place where we now have a venue with a huge circulation. Debbi can bring her people in, and it benefits her, her people, and us, so the positive flow is back and forth, as you can see. It is a wonderful synergy which is all due to networking. Now without having to run an entire showcase myself, I can create something big by sharing the spotlight with other people.

DEBBI: Thank you for illustrating such a beautiful point. Viki is a savvy, brilliant business woman for whom I have mad respect. I see what she has created in the world and was compelled to open the door to a conversation about what was possible, to explore alignment between us and what that might generate. Viki has been in business a long time. She is an amazing worker with a fabulous track record, and I found her to be super interesting and smart. I bring this up because I do not align myself with just anyone. If I align myself, it is with a winner. If I were to align myself with someone who is very green and just starting out, I would do so only to assist *them* and offer them my influence. I cannot look to do partner-type business with a beginner or we are both going to struggle. So if you are operating in your business at a high level, connect with others at your level and often even higher. We pull people up. Others pull us up. We support each other.

Co-create and collaborate at higher levels and find those savvy, brilliant beings who will be fun to play with in business. Viki is easy for me to play with as I know that when she says she is going to do something, she does it and then some. She is capable, on top of her business, and very knowledgeable. I find that joyful and again, have mad respect for her. Both of us responsibly responding in this way can open a lot of doors for profit and play. I like operating efficiently like that and you can produce the same. Just find where in your life there are existing relationships of importance and nurture them right now. Additionally, look around and create new relationships with those you look up to and who play a big, impressive game.

FREQUENTLY ASKED QUESTIONS:

AUTHOR: I have a question regarding the *New York Times* bestseller. Is there a different marketing avenue to get to that status? Is there a way to make a connection to someone to get them to read the book? How does that process work, because I heard Debbi say that she had a friend who put in a lot of money to get on that list. What is the process? Is that more of a networking and "who you know" type thing, or how does that happen?

VIKI: Becoming a *New York Times* best-selling author is about getting a formidable agency or agent to represent you and then getting signed by a New York publishing house. And then it is building up to a tremendous amount of book sales and most people do not have what it takes.

I have a friend who has written three *New York Times* bestsellers and now for her next books she only published through Amazon because she just could not justify the cost to run a *New York Times* bestseller launch anymore. Most people don't have the kind of financial numbers that are needed, so instead, they will hire a publicist and they will hire firms that will do the promotion for them, but the promotion has to be huge and it is expensive.

As Debbi and I both mentioned earlier, the process involves selling tons of books. Multiple book-selling venues are included in the final numbers for a one week *New York Times* book launch. When your book is sold through bookstores, if your books don't sell and they sit on a shelf, the bookstores will have it in your contract that any unsold books will be bought back by you. You have to have a lot of people around you, who are really well-positioned in that sphere, and achieving a *NYT* bestseller does not come cheap—that's the bottom line. I heard many spend in excess of a quarter of a million dollars.

The publishing world is changing, so if you have a bestseller or even better, Debbi and I both have multiple international bestsellers, then people will stand up and listen to you. They will look to you for your expertise, and your book does not have to be *New York Times bestseller*.

Amazon tracks book sales hourly for the bestsellers and that doesn't necessarily mean you are going to sell a million books. They base bestseller status on additional criteria that they will not reveal. We are not sure what the criteria is, but when we push a book to bestseller (and we are doing about two to three a week for other authors, and our own books), what we have found is that we just cover all the bases of everything we can possibly do to get attention drawn to that book. We manage all the activities that happen on Amazon, including correct positioning of the book, visits to the author's page and great reviews from a global audience. Again, Amazon won't share specifically what their algorithm is behind how they determine a bestseller so we cover all the bases for our authors.

We have had books that have gone bestseller with hundreds of dollars in book sales and we have had books that have gone bestsellers with thousands and thousands of dollars in book sales, so that will give you an idea of the range.

AUTHOR: I am on the fourth chapter of my book and you said that it is a good thing to go ahead and advertise your book before it is done so I am getting the cover completed and getting the name trademarked. I am using the great advice that you gave to set up a website for the book name. When is the best time to promote it before it is done? I am only in my fourth chapter, it has twelve chapters in the book, when will be a good time to start promoting it?

VIKI: For an advanced purchase, I don't think it should go out before a few months. I think people get tired of waiting if you have them wait too long, but it is never too early to have them engaged in your book and how it is developing in any way that you want to do that. We mentioned several specific ways in the last chapter. You start putting your book title and cover on your business card, put it on your website, say to your followers *it is coming soon,* add a blog to your website and talk about where you are going with your book. Get the book out there in social media, which can be done a year in advance. I think asking people to wait over sixty or ninety days when they paid money for the book might be stretching it. Debbi, what is your feeling about that?

DEBBI: I concur with what you are saying, and what I know about this business is that basically a tsunami gets created when you start promoting and talking about your book. So your book is the dream, and it really is a dream that flows out to your following. You want to build up to it with all the things that Viki just mentioned. Also, it is highly recommended to create little bookmarks, do your business cards, your website, and start letting people know about your book. I think one of the secrets to it is there has to be something in it for them. It not just *I am writing this book—check me out*. Rather it is sharing why the book's contents are beneficial to your potential audience. That is going to bring future readers in and get people engaged.

We have to involve people so they feel that there are reasons for them to read your book. And just so you know, there is a contingency of people out there who like to run advanced sale promotions, and there is an art to that. For the bestseller, create awareness of the book and excitement a few months before the bestseller launch, and then really drive sales on the launch date.

VIKI: With all of our books, we always donate a portion of the proceeds and sometimes the whole launch revenue goes to a charity. We have supported everything from the children in Africa to the blind to battered women's shelters. We adopted a child in the Dominican Republic and we are going to use the book profits and our own profits as publishers to continue to support this child until she is eighteen. Since it is not just a one-time donation, people love that and the media loves it. Everyone loves charities and the fact that you are doing a lot of good for the world.

DEBBI: The next chapter will be our final education about books before we move into the radio media interviews for authors. We are here to see you become successful, best-selling authors.

Discover More:
Become a Best-Selling Author and Radio PR Magnet
with Debbi and Viki in a comprehensive class:
BookRadio.Expert

Chapter Four
Your Book Launch
Propel Your Book to Success

DEBBI: You've got two experts from both sides of this field addressing this subject of becoming a best-selling author through self-publishing a book, as well as getting booked on radio shows free. We are going to give you as much information as possible, the full process for the book launch, including book reviews and book awards.

You are now putting the process together—you made it to the final installation of becoming a bestseller, the writing through the self-publishing of your book, and taking steps to turn your book into an international bestseller. There is no reason any more for self-hesitation about starting a book project in your life. You now know you have the ability to fulfill your wish to publish and you don't have to worry about starting something brand new. We know that taking your book to bestseller status is of huge importance to you.

Writing a book is a project that includes pouring your heart and soul into writing a masterpiece that is significant at this point in your life. Of course, there is also the matter of whether you will earn money from it and whether you will receive recognition from your book. Do understand that even seasoned authors wonder about this and thankfully what we are learning through this book is that it takes a little creativity and resourcefulness to propel your book to bestseller status. It is terrific that you are starting to take the steps that we are sharing here right away.

In this chapter of becoming a best-selling author, we are going to be discussing subjects like the formula for successful book launch, the big day that your book is launched, how to get your book reviewed, tracking book sales, getting support from those who surround you, good times to launch your book, secrets to becoming a best-selling author, book tours, bookstores, book awards plus solutions to success.

VIKI: I want to start out by talking about a **formula for a successful book launch**. Debbi was kind enough in the second chapter to give you an overview. Here, we are going to get more in depth with that subject and you also will receive a fabulous timeline for your book launch at the end of this chapter.

To start out, I would like to repeat some of the value and powerful benefits you receive when you become a best-selling author. **It definitely gives you credentials as an expert.** You are perceived as an expert even if you don't think you are a total expert. A best-selling book will solidify that niche for you. It raises the visibility of a book when a book gets the bestseller status, which often results in more orders and helps you spread your message globally as a general rule now, because so many books—almost all books, in fact, are available online.

In addition, becoming a best-selling author also results in **media interest** in you and more interview possibilities. Of course, over the next three chapters, Debbi is going to go into media, radio and interviews in much more depth to share with you how you can actually secure interviews and make being interviewed a success so that media people will invite you to come back again and again.

A bestseller often creates **more speaking engagement inquiries** and also enables you to secure higher fees for speaking arrangements. Most importantly, and I cannot stress this enough, **it opens doors for you.** There are so many ways that doors can be opened as a result of having a best-selling book. In light of that, I want to go into the steps and formula for doing a bestseller launch.

Step number one is to set specific goals. I will go into this in a little more detail since this is so important in everything you do in life. It is not just the book launch. Actually being able to set goals can open every kind of opportunity for you. You need to have a set plan of action about how you desire to go about generating the reality you really want to live so when you set goals for yourself, it is important that it is a goal that really motivates you.

You have to make sure that your goals are so important to you that you feel like you can't live without them and that there is tremendous value in achieving those goals—this will keep you on track and inspire you to work through the whole goal setting and accomplishment process. If you have little interest in the outcome or if your goals are irrelevant, if you know you can live without the goal, chances are putting in any work to make them happen are slim. Motivation is really the key to achieving goals in your life and I am sure many of you have found this to be true in the past with some of the goals that you've had. I will give you a formula on how to set goals in a way that works. Debbi specifically coaches on goal achievement. I coach as well, and I coach in really high pressure environments where there were millions of dollars on the line for projects and big teams involved in Fortune 500 and 100 companies.

Here are some of the highlights of what I have found to be the formula for successful projects of all kinds. You have to do everything with an *"I must do this"* attitude in order to make this goal a reality. If not, you're just going to feel disappointed and frustrated with yourself; you will feel as if you failed and there is no reason to do that. Not achieving a goal is very demotivating to everything in your life, not just the goal that you set. So remember to move forward with an *"I can do anything"* frame of mind. Be sure of the goal, make it motivating, and write it down: Why is your goal valuable to you? Also, share your goals with others and ask yourself, *"If I share my goals with others, what will I tell them to let them know that it is a worthwhile goal?"* Then you can use that value statement to motivate yourself even when you are not talking to others about your goal.

Number two is to set smart goals. When we say smart goals in coaching, it means they are **s**pecific, they are **m**easurable, they are **a**ttainable, they are **r**elevant and they are measured by **t**ime.

In order to set a **specific goal,** you have to be very clear and the goal has to be very well defined. Vague or generalized goals are not helpful because they don't provide the significant direction that you require to make your goals become a reality. You need goals to show you the way. Create an image in your mind and write down where you are heading so you know when you get there. It is a lot easier getting there if you know what the end looks like.

It is really important to also set **measurable goals**; therefore, you need to be precise about them. Describe your goals and set a timeline. This will help measure your success. If it is not measurable, you will never know whether or not you reach success and you will not feel fulfilled. So if you set very simple goals like "make my book a success," how do you know when the book is successful for you personally? Is it book sales? Is it the ability of the book to be distributed throughout different countries? Is it what the book might do for you? Is it that you want to develop different classes or programs, or that you want to open doors for yourself?

As we said earlier, you really need to know what that looks like so that you can measure results very specifically. This will help you know when you are successful and help you feel satisfied with the results. This is why I suggest that you define what success means to you.

Make sure your targets are attainable. For instance, this is your first book, you don't have an agent, you are not working with a publishing house, you desire to become a *New York Times* best-selling author, and sell a million books. Well, that may not be attainable right now from where you are at or with the funding that you have available.

It is important that you resist the urge to set targets that are really high. Yet, if you achieve something that you didn't have to work hard for, it is anticlimactic. It is not very satisfying. So you should aim for a mid-point.

I would also like to stress that when you are working, especially on your first book, you may think that this is *the* book, and as we said in the previous chapter, it could only be a portion of your story. If it is your whole story, it probably is too long and is not specific enough to be really successful. Look at this as possibly the start of your journey, especially if it is your first book, and make sure the goals for that first step are attainable. Even if it is your second or third book, you want to make sure you have attainable goals.

It is important for you to **analyze how your goals are relevant** to where you prefer your life and your career to be. What is the journey you are taking? What are the overall goals for your vision? You want to be able to set the goals for this and all projects relevant to the life journey that you have chosen.

Time is important in regards to goals. If you do not set deadlines on what you are doing, the book or the project can just go on and on and on. It is critical to have a sense of urgency. If you set a timeline, sometimes the achievement can come even quicker.

DEBBI: Having been through this process several times, I deeply appreciate the ideas you've presented, and when you are talking about having the discipline to execute action and strategy—that's the secret sauce. It really is because there are times when I, as an author, come up against my own resistance. Thoughts such as, *I don't want to work on my book today*, especially when it came to the proofing and editing before I turned it over to an editor. Resistance to committing to our book almost every day, I am sure is a known experience to us all. However, in order for the bestseller to happen, we do need to execute the strategy and take action anyway.

I suggest you take a deep breath and move forward. We always feel so much better on the other side when we move forward, knowing that we have accomplished something that day, and knowing that it is behind us. When you are launching a book, it is important to have sense of serenity about it, like *'this is what is next for me to do,'* and also be excited about what is waiting at the finish line. Ultimately you will be fine; just know you are not the first author to have a blockage. We all go through it. We have all been there and you will be part of the club. That's why we can have this conversation together. The bottom line is to try to make your book process as much fun as you can.

VIKI: I like to talk about setting goals in writing. I think Debbi, as a coach, will totally agree that the physical act of actually **writing down a goal** makes it more real and tangible for you. It is very important that you state your goals as something you will do, not as something you would like to do or might do. There is nothing nebulous about it; it is very direct. This goal you are aiming for is something you WILL DO.

Remember to **state your goal positively**. Don't use negative terms. Always approach something new from a creative state. You want to picture your book project as ideal so that it is motivating for you. When you look at your goal, is it so positive that it just makes you want to fly?

A to-do list is also helpful. You may want to make a to-do list template that has your goals on the top of it. I post my goals all over the place—on mirrors with sticky pads, so that I am looking at it while I am brushing my teeth and doing other daily routines. If your goal is stated positively, it will inspire you and move you into a feeling that you have achieved it, like you are there, you are living in the result. So the journey becomes an experience that is getting you to where you are already living emotional and spiritually.

Another part of goal setting is **making an action plan,** and so many times this is missed. You know you have to plan all the steps you require along the way. I was interviewing Marcia Wieder, best-selling author and founder of Dream University. She said that it is really important when you first have your dream, and this is true with your book, to not get too specific with whether or not you can create it or with very specific strategy steps, because sometimes that can squelch or limit your dreams. As you move on in the process, you have to get really focused because you have to put the steps in place in order to get where you are going.

As I mentioned earlier, Debbi has a wonderful timeline which we share at the end of this chapter that will help you with the details, and you can adjust that to what's comfortable for you. Keep a list nearby you each day that keeps you moving, and as you go through the list and are able to cross off different targeted individual action items, you can celebrate along the way. You don't have to wait until the end. Be really joyful about the fact that you have achieved a portion of what you need to achieve in order to arrive at the end result.

It is important that you **stick with it**. It is an ongoing activity, not just a means to an end. It is not just a beginning and an end. You need to keep yourself on track and you need to make regular time slots available in your calendar to review your goals and your destination. Even though it may seem really clear, you need to be looking at it every day. Find that sticky note or whatever works so it is in front of your face, and you can start really living that reality. This practice will encourage you to stick with it, not forget or put it aside for a week or a month or a year.

I have done that with some projects. I first had the idea of doing a magazine probably three decades ago and I wanted to do it in the worst way. I knew exactly how it would look. But it didn't come to fruition for decades and decades until finally the timing was right. Advanced technology allowed us to do it in a much better way than would have been available decades ago. It was something I put on the back burner because I didn't have a strategic plan for it as I was busy doing other things.

When I did develop a tight plan for the magazine, it happened overnight and we got people like Jack Canfield and Marcia Wieder and Marshall Goldsmith in the first few issues. It was amazing to me what and who we attracted once I had a set goal in my mind, and when I first talked to some of these people, it wasn't even a reality yet. We had a date set for when we were going to have the first issue of the magazine out, and I at least had plans in place. Earlier, when I had no plans in place, nothing came to fruition, so a mindset of attraction is really important.

One of the things that I think is also significant is **accepting personal responsibility.** You know you are the person that is the most intimate with your book so you can't depend on a publishing company; you can't depend on outside people to pull everything together for you. With your book, you need to be the focal point of what's happening. I am not saying you can't outsource because outsourcing is a wonderful thing. Things that you don't know how to do or you don't care to learn to do, you can certainly outsource. You just need to be the person that drives the project; you need to assume the marketing role for your book because no one knows it better than you do. No one can be a better spokesperson for your book than you. No one has more at stake than you do for the best results for your book.

Make a target list of possible endorsers. Think of what you can provide to them and start building relationships in advance.

Another thing that helps make your launch successful is to **engage your tribe and your followers early on.** Do proactive things such as giving away portions of your book as blog posts and request engaged suggestions. Start a group in social media as you're working through your book so people feel that they have some ownership in your book. It is essential that you engage people early in the process and include them in the excitement and momentum as it builds.

One of the most helpful things you can do (especially if you have a small list or maybe even a nonexistent list) is the idea of **forming a launch team** for support. You might say, "If I have no list, how do I do this?" Weeks before the actual launch date, you can write an invitation on social media and share that you are going to create a special group. This group will have unique privileges for your launch. Let them know some of the benefits you can offer them. They may include a copy of the e-book before publication. You can start a Facebook group where only people that are in this elite group and are helping with the launch have access. It costs nothing to do that on Facebook. You can also offer them a discount on one of your courses as an incentive for joining the launch with you and really create some excitement. Perhaps they get expanded access to you or to your team members. Offer them a bonus teleseminar if you have that type of product—something that will be a great learning experience for them.

In return, **ask them to write a short review on Amazon** when your book comes out to help spread the word, especially during the week of the launch.

Social media mentions are fabulous. As an example, my company has a book that we are launching this week and as of last night, when I got the report from our team, it was a bestseller in all categories in three countries. I shared the success on social media. My friends and fans also shared. Then, this morning when I got up and I checked the status myself, the book had gone number one bestseller in all categories in six countries and two of those countries are not

English as first language countries. I shared again the book's progress and success. That is the kind of excitement that spreading the word can build. And there's strength in numbers when many people are posting to social media.

You can also **brainstorm and share ideas on calls** as to how the team might get expanded exposure for the message to an even greater audience. Group calls will also create a learning experience for those that are helping you with your book.

These are just some of the exciting ways to build a following if you don't already have one. Believe me, we have a fantastic board of book reviewers and advisors at our Bestselling Authors International Organization—they help us move these bestsellers all over the world as a result of their following and spreading the word. Engaging people is really powerful.

I am a big supporter of not doing advance sales. We advise all of our authors that we move to bestseller not to do this because when you have advanced sales, you can sometimes have the book be off its timing on launch day.

We always **try to get all the sales on the first day.** The book that I was just speaking about earlier is now a number one bestseller in all categories in six countries. That book broke yesterday and this morning when I got up at four in the morning it had hit number one already. That's because the author cooperated with us, did not do any promotion on her side until launch day. On Amazon, the book's ratings change every hour. The more consistent and the more penetrating the purchases are, the more buyers are driven to visit and purchase on the book's site, the higher the ratings and that may propel you to Hottest New Release in addition to bestseller. When readers buy within a short period of time, it will increase your opportunity to reach your bestseller goal.

Now a particular book I'll refer to here received tremendous reviews. The author is a medical doctor, and it is a book that is not just directed to patients, but also other medical doctors. The book is about how to renew excitement about being a doctor and what that means to the patient community. The author had some medical journals that wrote up the book and people posted a lot of reviews of the book—sixty-one reviews on Amazon U.S. People purchased and reviewed the book very early because some of the journals broke early. Sometimes you can't help that. This author got so many reviews—all five stars—but we still have not made it to the top-rated book yet on Amazon because these reviews were spread out over such a long period of time.

We promote two to three new bestsellers a week and we know that this works so I would advise you to try to choreograph everything so it all comes in at the same time. **We do the same thing with our press release and video distribution.** If we are going to launch a book on Monday, we send out our press release on Friday. It impacts Google ratings for the book and the author in a most positive way.

Another thing, **be sure your profile is on Amazon Author Central.** It is important because when you put your profile on Amazon Author Central it connects to your book page, along with your photo and bio. There is also some great reporting ability that appears on that site. Don't miss the opportunity to set up that Author page before your book breaks. Sometimes it takes a little while for it to show up so you have to coordinate the page at least a few days early. Just as you are posting your book on Amazon Kindle or as a paperback, you should be establishing your Amazon Author Central profile about the same time and make sure it is connected. They won't connect your book until your book is approved on Amazon, so it has to be a coordinated effort.

DEBBI: I want to offer a point of view that came from a very well-known self-published author, Guy Kawasaki. You might know of Guy, a very well-known gentleman who speaks all over the world. He was at an annual book conference and he was giving advice to authors. He said, "Publish your book yourself."

Now this is a guy who can go to any publishing house and get a deal. There is a reason he said what he did. Guy Kawasaki, who has authored twelve books, said to the book attending audience, "For many people, self-publishing may still have a negative connotation, so I would like to substitute a new term: 'artisanal publishing.'" Guy suggested that self-publishing should be viewed more like small batch wine makers and other modern craftsmen.

He advocated an entrepreneurial approach to authorship. He said, "Listen, I would happily return to traditional publishing if a publisher would offer me an enormous advance, say two million. But let's be real, most book advances are only a tiny fraction of that." Guy believes there are better ways to raise money than "sucking up to a New York publisher for nine months." That's a big deal for an author of his stature to share from the stage. What I am sharing with you is that some of you may think, "I am a small potato, nobody knows about me; I am not an expert in my niche." This is just not true. I am sharing a real story about a well-known leader who has already put out twelve books, and he himself will only self-publish to a best-selling launch.

Guy also offered a couple of tips that were noteworthy for self-publishing. I got this from his key note where he said, "Write for the right reasons." "The wrong reasons," he said, "were to make money, to get famous, or boost your company's visibility or sales. The right reasons are to have something meaningful to say. Perhaps you want to further a cause, you want to meet an intellectual challenge, and, of course, most of us are going to make money. We may get a little more famous, we may help our company by publishing a book or through entrepreneurship. But the core of why we should be writing a book is if we have a unique experience or perspective that will enrich people's lives."

Writing a book is about passion. It is because you have something to say, you need to say it so much, and you need to put it on paper so it has an evergreen life. The next thing that Guy suggested was to use the best tools. He felt that Microsoft Word, software I work with, is at the top of his list of tools that a self-publisher can and should be using. It is an industry standard for word processing and using Word makes it easy when you are selling your book on Amazon and CreateSpace. When you use Microsoft Word, it creates formatting changes for you so easily.

The next suggestion is to get help from the crowd, your followers, friends, colleagues, and database. You don't necessarily have to hide your work from the world until it is something that you feel is truly worthy. Guy felt that writing a book can tap into the crowd at critical stages, and he uses his social media followers for critiques of his book outline. Guy does this by creating a Google document which is viewable by others, but only he can make changes.

Additionally, Guy asks for volunteers to edit the first draft of his manuscript. I just want to say right off the top that is pretty brilliant because I myself have suffered through several edits of my own book. I always make sure I do a minimum of three to five edits by myself before I turn it over to a professional editor. I wanted the professional editor to edit my book when it was worthy of being published; it still came back from the editor with lots of amazing changes and things I hadn't caught.

I love the fact that Guy puts this out to people for getting points of view and volunteer edits, wherein people are basically doing the work for you and coming up with things that you might not think of. There are so many extraordinary people out there who are happy to get involved. The bottom line of all this information from Guy Kawasaki that I think is noteworthy is that he only recommends self-publishing and utilizing some easy tools to get authors ahead. It's very creative or "artisanal" stuff.

VIKI: That is fabulous, Debbi. Thank you so much for that insight. I love the credibility that Guy is giving to self-publishing because it is such a wonderful opportunity we have now that we didn't have five or ten years ago—an arena now wide open for authors to get their stories out. I appreciate the concept that it becomes so easy and to have someone of Guy Kawasaki's credibility removes any stigma from self-publishing is a wonderful thing. Thank you so much for sharing this important information.

LAUNCH DAY

I'm going to now address the big day that your book is launched and what to expect. Debbi, by all means, I would love for you to add to this because we both have been through different experiences with the big launch day.

The first thing is to **send reminders in the morning** to your following. We have a following all over the world, and we send out the reminders to people at different times. Sometimes the day before because some of our people may be in the Pacific Rim, some people are in Australia, and some are over in Europe. We time when we send out the reminders so that everyone will come in about the same time, or as close to the same time as possible. For the U.S., we send early in the morning and then we monitor the standings that appear in the location of your book review area. When you run your launch, you need to do the same thing.

Ratings are right above the book reviews and it is where all the information about your book is, including the ISBN number, who the publisher is, and so forth. Nothing will show up until your book comes within the first hundred in its category. Once it does that, it will start showing your standings. Therefore, you need to **monitor book ranking hourly and take screen shots,** which are proof of its standing. I think I may have mentioned it before, and it is really important: Amazon does not keep track of the standings so there is nowhere you can find it after the fact. If you miss it, you miss it. When we are launching books, we have a member of our team rotate and monitor the book that is launched around the clock. Someone is in charge of going in hourly, all through the night, twenty-four hours a day, for forty-eight hours, sometimes up to three days, to keep monitoring if the book is still moving. Track your book, take screen shots of where that book is as it is moving up, and take screen shots of your book's rankings in all countries.

We have a book that we will be launching on Thursday from a doctor in Singapore about toxic substances and how they affect our health. Because Singapore doesn't have a dedicated Amazon group like Italy, Australia, Canada or the U.S., we will be monitoring all of the countries for him because people who are on his list are from everywhere, even the people in Singapore who will be supporting his launch will be using different Amazon sites to purchase his book from different geographic areas. You have to go in and look at that particularly if you have a global audience and are going for global sales and international bestseller status.

When you are using social media to promote your book, there could be a number of people in other countries where you don't actually have a lot of fans, but they are attracted to your book. Perhaps they start buying the book and doing reviews, and your book becomes a bestseller in that country. You will never know it unless you monitor it yourself and you will never have proof of it unless you take screen shots so this is a really important point to remember.

Post your stats, as they come in, on your social media. Let people know and then ask for help to promote your book. Say, "My book just reached number 86 on the bestseller list, but I am really trying to make it to number one. Can you help me?" This is really great as it helps spread the word and makes the book more successful, and your fans and following can be a part of it. It is just a wonderful and exciting way to keep in touch.

Needless to say, and I am sure Debbi can attest to this, launch day and the days before and the days after can be very busy if you are doing it on your own. When you are doing a bestseller book launch yourself, you need to block out the time and really dedicate yourself to this process because all of this is very key to the success for your book.

DEBBI: I have a very funny story to tell you. I was so green when I did my first bestseller launch. I have a friend who is well-known as an expert and teacher for creating bestsellers. My book was ready for the first day of its launch and my friend Teresa calls me and confers with me. I tell you, I was so excited about the day of my book launch and I shared with Teresa, "Wow, I worked so hard on this book for so long. I have taken steps every single day and I am ready for the big day. So tomorrow for my big bestseller launch day, I am thrilled because I just booked myself a manicure and pedicure. I also booked myself a massage. Boy, do I deserve this! I am so excited to finally take it easy." Teresa was steadying herself on the other end of the line.

"Oh my goodness," she laughed, "I want you to take a seat and ground yourself. Tomorrow is not the day to have a massage and a mani-pedi. Your launch day is the day you are on high alert. This is the day you are manning your computer. This is the day, if you have a team, your team is on high alert, too. You have got to watch your rankings and your numbers throughout the day and night—pay attention, pay attention. This is the day you are going to become a bestseller; this is the day you have been working for.

Don't sit back and let it happen; you are in it to win it. In fact, while the launch is going on, keep sending out updates to all your influencers who have agreed to help you on the book campaign. Send out the copy that you provided, along with the Facebook blurbs, the tweets, the LinkedIn posts, the newsletters–create an excitement so everybody is talking about it. Also send out updates, like the screen shots, which you can post on your website, your Facebook fan page, and any site where your book is being supported." So needless to say, I cancelled all my luxury body and nail appointments the day of my book launch. Instead I stayed home and manned the computer and I became a first time Best-Selling Author! It was worth it!! Funny story, right?

On the day of your book launch, you will set your alarm for early in the morning (after midnight is best) and know that from that time to the very end of the evening, you will be watching your book's sales and rankings in every country. Take your dinner and a little bit of sleep and then wake up the next morning to do it again. That's your life for the next couple of days; it is an exciting train to be on and you want to be involved and hands on for the ride.

It is like seeing the stock you invested in go up and at some point, your stock is going to hit. As your book becomes number one, you want to be cognizant and present for that moment: taking the screen shots, being thoroughly involved with what is happening and definitely have the bottle of champagne in the refrigerator ready to open and celebrate for the big moment.

VIKI: Absolutely. Authors should monitor the updates many times per day and you will get so excited. The author I was talking about earlier, the doctor, was actually working at her practice and she would send me messages throughout the day like, "Oh, my goodness I can't believe this." We keep authors updated so that they can get enthusiastic and they can be a part of the launch when we send the emails to let them know where the book is and we send them screen shots as proof. The excitement keeps building and building.

Another thing that you can do is something I learned from a very successful author. He launched his book and during the launch **offered people one-hour interviews and conference calls.** During the hour, he went into Amazon and kept **giving book updates** with stats and sharing them on the call. This was amazing! It was a great teaching opportunity where he shared pieces of wisdom in his book. I learned a lot in the course of that hour and you better believe I jumped on the Kindle site and ordered his book—so did everyone who was on that call. I am sure that was one of many calls and interviews he did during the day where he kept reporting where the book stats were during the call. It was really, really powerful. I was totally susceptible to the excitement and consequently I bought his book without any question.

At the end, **celebrate your success.** It is really important, and don't celebrate it alone. Be sure to let everyone who has helped you, everyone out on social media, all of your following, let them know how your book launch is going. When they find out how well the book's doing, they might jump in and get involved even more, put the word out and continue the success of the book launch.

We have had launches where the success of the book continued to accelerate through countries and through numbers for up to four days and that's a long time for a launch team to be checking the ratings every hour. If you keep the excitement going, it is amazing what can happen.

DEBBI: I want to share a website. Go to your computer right now as I share this. Go and open a browser right now and type in NovelRank.com. What you will find is this site provides **free Amazon sales rank tracking**, book sales on Amazon, and rankings for Kindle e-books and Printed Editions.

It is a completely free website for tracking books or other products on Amazon. What is beautiful about it is it gives the information for the United States and for the U.K., and it also provides book tracking for Canada, France, Germany, Japan, China, Italy, Spain, and India. It is terrific and gives you charting for real time data. It displays sales ranking, so when your book is up and ready, get signed up on that site. I recommend you have several browsers open simultaneously. You could have your Amazon page open at the same time so you can watch your ranking.

During the best-selling launch of my second book, I was assisted once again by Teresa, the same friend I referred to before, who called me and asked, "How are you doing?" We can get so myopic when we are in the middle of our own bestseller campaign, so I found it to be loving and nurturing to have people call and check in on me who are good at this, because they reminded me of little pieces that might be forgotten. This friend of mine called when I was deep into the launch for my second book, and seeing that my book had become a bestseller, she asked, "Honey, how is your book doing in other countries?"

Well, I was so busy checking the U.S. that I had completely forgotten about checking my rankings in other countries. When Teresa called, I immediately started checking by opening the Canadian Amazon page and found that my book was a bestseller there, as well. Then I started going into the other websites to see what was going on in other countries, and in multiple countries, indeed I was also a #1 bestseller.

If you want to keep it easy, check everything with plenty of time by being in front of the computer to see what's happening and also keep open NovelRank.com so you can watch what's happening throughout the world in real time. That's also how you can see your sales on a daily or monthly basis on this terrific site.

VIKI: If you want to get information directly for Amazon or distribution pages, you can go to Author Central where there is sales information. When you set up your own book on

Kindle KDP (Kindle Direct Publishing) with Amazon, there is a tab called "Reports." They are not always up to date, but will give some idea what money is coming in.

We encourage you to **price your Kindle book at 99 cents,** and when you direct everything towards Kindle, not your paperback, Amazon will link your Kindle and your paperback together if you have both, so readers have easy access to either. When you sell the Kindle version of your book for 99 cents, your royalties on that are not going to be extremely high. Royalties are 35% at low pricing that only run during the launch for maybe two to three days, but it gives people great incentive to buy your e-book. (You receive 70% royalties when you sell your Kindle e-book for between $2.99 and $9.99).

If you are doing heavy advertising, I recommend that you advertise that this Kindle book is only going to be **marked down to 99 cents for twenty-four hours**. You need to leave the Kindle at 99 cents for two or three days because people don't always check their emails the same day and some people will get frustrated if they take (late) action and the price is already raised, so give them a little bit of a chance to buy the book if they have not checked their email on the day of your launch. If the book breaks on Monday or Tuesday, I recommend giving people until Wednesday or Thursday before you end the sale. Keeping the Kindle for a few days at 99 cents is worth the reduction of the royalties for the bestseller launch only because it creates a frenzy when you reduce the price.

DEBBI: What Viki suggests here is to keep the 99 cents price up for only a couple of days, and when it hits bestseller status and you pass the forty-eight to seventy-two hour mark, you then return the Kindle back to the regular, full price.

VIKI: The good times to launch a book? Tuesdays, Wednesdays, and Thursdays are usual the best days, although we have launched books every day of the week with success.

Make sure that when you are launching your book, it is not something you are doing as a side activity. As Debbi mentioned earlier, don't have a lot going at the time of your launch; don't do it while other projects are happening. If you have joint venture partners or affiliates and you know that they are going to be helping with the launch, or they are going to be busy with mailings, as your biggest partners, try to find out if they can put focus on your book during your launch day, too. Time your book in a way that it is not conflicting with their planned activities so your partners can help you to the ultimate outcome. Don't schedule your book launch during a time that you have a lot going on because the week you are launching your bestseller is going to be a full time, all-consuming activity for at least a few days.

We talked a little bit about this and the fact that there are **Amazon sections in 13 different countries** where you can secure bestseller status, including Japan, Australia, Europe and Mexico, so if you want to become an international bestseller, one of the really important things that you can do using social media is to start befriending people that are in these other locations as part of your plan.

Get to know them and ask them what you can do for them six months before your book comes out, four months before your book comes out, and then when your book is getting ready to launch, you can ask them to support your book and will have a good foundation. In these other countries, you have to do business or have connections and you can do it through social media. You can do it through various vertical marketing blogs and different associations that may be interested in your book subject matter and have a global audience.

Try to foster those relationships in at least a few countries with a few people so ultimately they will send out to their readership to increase the chance that you might go international bestseller. Since you have done this several times, Debbi, do you have other suggestions for fostering international interest in the book?

DEBBI: You know part of it depends on what your reach is and who you are engaged with. Because of the media work that I do, the exposure received from my speaking and teaching, from becoming a best-selling author, I am often interviewed in various media venues, which in turn has created me being connected with people in various countries. We follow each other and do our best to stay involved in what each other is doing. These are the influencers we all want to be connected with. I also recommend **using newsworthy press releases to increase your reach.**

I highly recommend press releases, and to create a good press release, it is very important to either know how to do it professionally or pay someone to do it for you. Learn how to write a correct press release, because the press release company will deny a press release if it hasn't been written correctly.

Perhaps the headline isn't correct, or the subtitle, or the body. There is only one reason to write a press release: it has to be newsworthy. A press release is not about me, me, me, buy my book, I just wrote a book - a sales thing. It really has to have content in it that people desire to read. I would have a strategy and create an action plan. An action plan is something you take out and every day you do something from your strategy plan list.

On my action plan, I included press releases. One of the press releases I wrote was in advance of my book, which included a lot of content in my niche on key ways to create goals and dreams. Educational and statistical ideas that people hadn't heard of before to illustrate points is very powerful.

The press release was written in advance so the first press release might be picked up worldwide and people would find out about my book for its launch. I also prewrote a second press release, which was at the ready for the moment I actualized becoming a best-selling author. The moment being a bestseller was a reality, I submitted the prewritten press release, noting that my book had just become a bestseller. During the launch process, it is too much to write a release on those days. It is advised to have it all done in advance, and at the ready so you just press the send button to submit your release when you hit number one.

So again, prewrite a press release. It can go worldwide and create a lot of interest in other countries that might not otherwise have known about you, the author, and your book. Those are a few suggestions.

VIKI: Really great suggestions. A couple more things that I think are important I will very briefly mastermind with you here.

The first thing is **plan virtual book tours**. This is a strategy that works so well you can do this on your own. You can research different people who are doing interviews and doing blogs; I would recommend that you search the web for someone to host your virtual book tour on blogs. You can do this starting with a weekly price, as little as twenty-five dollars. Some of the places that provide these services for virtual book tours are inexpensive so do a search on the web as there are many of them out there and some of them are very vertical, from the standpoint of the type of books that they promote. You are going to be busy enough and this is something you can get off your plate pretty inexpensively.

Radio book tours can also be powerful. I have friends who are really good at what they do; they usually book radio tours. Debbi is an expert in that arena and will give you a lot of information over the next three chapters on how to do this yourself. If you prefer to hire someone to do this for you instead, it is not going to be under one hundred dollars; it is going to be high hundreds to thousands of dollars. It also may be worth considering as it is great to have radio interviews locked in. Then all you have to do is show up comfortably in your office or in your home and be able to do an interview from your telephone and be very productive in driving a lot of people to your book.

Another thing I wanted to mention is **working with bookstores**. There are a number of different ways to work with bookstores. We love Amazon's CreateSpace and the reason we love CreateSpace so much is because they have expanded distribution where people can actually go into bookstores and request your book. The bookstore can actually go into catalogues and order your book for the reader through CreateSpace.

If you actually want to go through the trouble of developing a relationship with a particular bookstore, it is important that you promote your book to this store, especially if you promoted it to bestseller and the bookstore feels it is a relevant book. You can work out a consignment deal.

Usually with a deal, you get a small percentage of the money that comes in from the book and you have to agree to take books back if they don't sell. You can also go in to the bookstore and help them become aware of your books from distributors like from CreateSpace so that they can order the book. You can then direct people to go in and order the book.

I have a quick story. I don't know if any of you know this or not, but there was an author out there who had some success by the name of Wayne Dyer. When Wayne's first book was published, no one was buying the book. That was ages ago, when everything was traditional publishing. They were just going to take it out of print so Wayne said, "Well how many books would have to be purchased in order to not have it go out of print?" The number they gave him was five thousand or so.

He bought those books. He created a publishing name, had the books delivered with that publishing name to his garage, and he took his kids for a cross-country tour and pitched that book to bookstores along the way. At the time, Wayne had a pretty large family, and they would all call the bookstores in the next city they were going to the day before and request the book. They would all call in at different times and say, "Gee, I heard about this new book by Wayne Dyer. Do you have it?"

And the bookstore would say, "No, we don't; no, we don't know about it." They would have so many inquiries from his family calling that when Wayne showed up the next day and said he would like to make a deal putting his books in the store, they said, "Oh, we had all these calls for this book. Of course we will!" So that's just a little fun story about how Wayne Dyer achieved unbelievable success. I don't even know how many bestsellers he had before he passed on; he is one of my favorite authors and I think it is great story of how, with perseverance and the desire to move forward, you can do anything.

Now it is a lot easier to do that because you have distributors like CreateSpace. The bookstores can just order directly from them and you can also encourage friends and people within your local bookstores and community to go in and ask for your book. That will encourage the bookstores to order the book and carry it. I hope you enjoyed that story. I like that story because I appreciate Wayne Dyer so much as an author. It is important that you are always professional and respectful, even if the bookstore tells you to come pick up your books because they are not selling. That is part of the deal if you want to go the bookstore route.

I personally think authors do very well with online circulation of their books, and you don't necessarily have to have a book with store presence anymore to experience success. If that's important to you, you can make that happen, but remember that there are potentially going to be tons of books returned to you from the bookstores. You may have that second or third book in you, so you need to keep a good relationship with these bookstores since you want them to welcome you back.

There is so much that can be done with online purchasing with a book, and there are so many e-book distribution places. I think I said this earlier, but I should mention Smashwords again. Now they are very picky about their formatting and they require an ePub in order for you to submit your e-book and you might need to get help on this. They send this out to really valuable distribution units that have to do with getting books store exposure for your iBook, The Nook, etc. I think it is really important to look at Smashwords, too, as a secondary distribution source.

DEBBI: Many people will come up against this as an old-fashioned way of thinking. I often find with book launches that people, just because they don't know better, will say to me, as I'm an author, "When will you be doing a book tour across the country?" However, almost everything now is virtual, as opposed to the old model of physically travelling the country or world to offer bookstore signings. You can still do the old model - it does still exist. It's important to know that this can be very effectively done virtually. You can do a virtual book tour through Skype calls or Google Hangouts. You can make little movie video trailers about your book, giving away content, which takes just minutes to reach out to your potential readers.

Where I lived in California, there was a notable bookstore and scheduling a book signing there is quite a big deal. They request that you give people a workshop, along with your book signing, so I did that and it was tremendous, I have to say. I was told that often for book signings, a lot of people do not show up. I can't tell you why; however, I did really, really well for my workshop and book signing. In fact, I ended up doing two back-to-back workshops because there were so many people attending and I ended up connecting with readers I would have never met otherwise because I sold and signed books. It was really fun for me to do and in all honesty, in my overall book campaign, I don't think it made a lick of a difference as to whether I became a bestseller or not.

The book signing did not influence my numbers in that way. What it did do is place my book in a prestigious and well-attended L.A. bookstore, and give me a presence there as an author. What it did do was allow me to create and present a workshop about my book, my work, and my expertise. It did allow me to do a signing and meet new readers and followers. If an event like this suits your soul, then set up a local or non-local book signing and make an event out of it.

You may want to thank people in person for supporting you and your book, or meet and greet new or already known-to-you people. Folks who are your friends and family, who have been watching and assisting you through the campaign may desire a gathering to celebrate the book's accomplishment! Absolutely do the book signing and know it is in no way essential to you becoming a best-selling author; it doesn't have to be part of your action plan.

VIKI: Absolutely. I completely agree. In addition, I want to cover three more areas that are important to be aware of and you may already be, but I would like to shine some light on them. Book awards: do they matter? Yes, they matter. We enter all of our books that we do for ourselves, all of my personal books and our anthologies into book award contests, and we have been awarded with every single one of our books. It makes a big difference when you have a bestseller *and* an award-winning book. It is really impressive to have your book be a number one international bestseller and an award winner. It's really impressive.

Book award institutions charge a fee to enter the contest; it is usually nominal if you get in early—about fifty dollars. The cost goes up to sometimes one hundred dollars. You should research on the web what book award you are interested in, what's the best step for your book, and which book awards have a good reputation. I would highly recommend this.

Book fairs are a wonderful place to meet all kinds of agents, other writers, directors, and editors. If you pick the right book fair (they are all over the world, and they are happening all year long), it is a terrific place to network. You may be able to pitch your book, if you want to go a more traditional publishing route. Certainly, it will give your book some exposure and you can meet some people who might help you, if nothing else, with endorsements for your next book. It is a great place for authors to network and then stay on top of book and author news. Search out some of your favorite places for book fairs. There will be authors and publishers you can meet who are in the Literary Guild.

DEBBI: Certainly I concur on **the import of book reviews and on awards**. It has changed my life as an author. First of all, my *becoming* an author was a huge surprise to start with. I talk to authors all the time who say, "Writing a book and being an author is my calling. I know I have to write something." Au contraire for me! I was very surprised to have any desire to write. Writing a book dropped into my space and once I started to write my first book, I became very passionate to put words on paper or digitize my story. Just as curious as my becoming an author was the end result of becoming a best-selling author, and on my second book, an international best-selling author. Being a best-selling author has really changed the professional game for me and I highly recommend it.

Recently, my second book received a wonderful review from the judges at *Writer's Digest*. *Writer's Digest* has a big panel of judges who read and write independent reviews on your book and give their top reviewed books a rating. They comment on everything from the book cover, to the book font, the book's content, the punctuation and grammar, and then what kind of book you have written within your category, and whether or not they would recommend your book to others. When you address having book reviews, I say full steam ahead, because I personally have received a couple of reviews from outstanding review sources and these are reviews you can use to promote your book further and post on your web page and sundry sites that support your book. You may be interviewed in media, and you can use a quote from a book review. You may end up using quotes from the book reviews on your next published book and next book after that. These reviews have lives of their own. Book reviews utilize book experts who read and rank your book in your book's category as well as recommending (or not recommending) your book. It is good, honest feedback.

When you receive that independent review back and hopefully see their accolades, it is a big deal. You spent so much time writing, drafting, editing, rewriting your book, it should be reviewed once it's published. Again, you can use a little quote your book received, or even a huge paragraph. To do this, you want to look at venues like *Publishers Weekly*; you want to look at reviewing sites like *Writer's Digest, U.S. Book Review, USA Today*, and the *San Francisco Chronicle*. You should have a strong pitch since they will ask you for very specific book information each time you submit your book for potential reviews and awards. The good news is once you submit your book for a review or an award; you will understand in general what the setup is and what is required for each award site. I highly recommend following through on awards and reviews as it increases the longevity for your book and can cause new readers to notice it.

I don't know how you buy books, but I actually read reviews, and those book reviews will determine for me whether I purchase a book. There are so many books to choose from, and rather than take a crapshoot on whether a book will be enjoyable for me to read or not, I read lots of reviews and choose my next book that way. Do you see how your book having a beautiful review can increase readership? Also, you can post a great book review or book award everywhere, including your Author Page, your Amazon book page, your fan page, etc. You can also use any great quotes in your bios and resume. That can beef up your sales as well as the interest in how your book is doing.

I also want to address the unthinkable, what people don't usually say or talk about on subjects like this when they teach about books and radio and media. So let me bring it up. What if you *don't* reach bestseller status? What if you don't hit the bestseller list on your launch day? Here's the answer. You can go out and start selling enough books in the coming weeks, like one week at a time, one day at a time, and you can work to still land yourself on the bestseller list. In other words, just because it did not happen on launch day, it can still happen if you put action steps into it.

You can re-implement a couple of new things. For instance, you can try to land major media placement, such as TV, magazines, or radio that could cause a sudden swell of interest in your book. Secondly, you can kick off a fresh bestseller campaign and go after the bestseller title once more. Please know all of what's possible. I am not saying that this will happen to you, but if it should, if you miss the mark, don't get weighed down and stop the process out of disappointment or frustration. If becoming a best-selling author doesn't quite happen on your big day, you will know what you can do to move forward anyway. It is important to learn from what went wrong so you can correct those steps.

Maybe you didn't have enough campaign partners aligned with you. Maybe you missed doing a lot of the actions steps you wanted to commit to, and you are feeling the *ouch* of poor results. On the big launch day, always stay around in front of your computer and by the telephone. The bottom line is that something went awry and there is a reason you did not become a bestseller, so pick a new date, create a new bestseller campaign, and go for it!

FREQUENTLY ASKED QUESTIONS:

AUTHOR: Since my book came out in February, and taking account of all the recommendations that you both shared, I'm looking at what kind of things I can do now even though my book came out a few months ago to really promote it.

VIKI: We move books to bestseller even when they have been on Kindle or on Amazon for a long time, when we do a refresher launch. We have one author who lives in Australia and her book was published eight years ago, but it was evergreen, so it could be re-launched with bestseller status in mind. We moved it to bestseller successfully. You can breathe some fresh air into a book; it is never too late to do that with a book unless your book is dated and its information is no longer relevant.

You can also apply all the principles that were given in this book to make it happen. You can do that at any time; it is just amazing. We did a book for a leadership coach and that book went bestseller about eight years ago. We just relaunched her campaign to bring some fresh air in the book because she developed a course that she attached to it as part of her platform now. So she wanted to reignite interest in the book to enhance the course.

There are a lot of different ways you can do it, and I want to stress and I know Debbi will agree with me, we have given you a lot of information and what is important here is to take what applies to what you want to do. Don't get overwhelmed with the ideas. We have given a lot of people a lot of information in this book. Take the things that really appeal to you and pull those out and use them and then keep the rest for later as they may come in hand for another time.

AUTHOR: Thank you so very much because I am interested in developing a platform and using my book to create messages and even developing a workbook and things of that nature. I am looking at different avenues to take my book and reach my readers and audience on a more profound level.

VIKI: That's what Debbi and I like to hear because that is what a book is all about—the development of a platform. You are on such a wonderful track there.

DEBBI: I am in accordance with Viki's statement—that's what books can open up for us when we use different strategies to reach a positive outcome.

One point to remember is that not all books are evergreen. Evergreen means the information contained in the book is not for that moment only or the time it is actually published; rather, it is information that anybody can pick up at any time, start reading, and it will apply. If your book is evergreen, you can definitely recreate a book launch. Sometimes all it takes is aligning with new launch partners, and it is a done deal. Sometimes all you want to do is change the book cover, give it a refreshing, new look or make other minor changes for good impact. I want to remind everybody about your excitement for your book and how putting your book out there is exciting.

Books change lives every moment. Everybody's book is unique. It is unlike any other media. What is amazing about this world of being an author is many people try to write a book and truthfully only a few follow through and succeed. If you even completed your book, you are part of a small exclusive group of people in the world, so kudos to you. Authoring a book enables you to spread your message and broaden your horizons beyond your wildest dreams.

Being an author and publishing your book is a very surprising journey. When you take this experience in earnest to say, "I am doing this. I am going to become a best-selling author," you will find doors opening for you in ways you could not have predicted. Being a two-time best-selling author has absolutely changed my life personally and professionally. I am doing things; I have been afforded opportunities I couldn't have predicted before launching my books. The same can be true for you, too.

Next, I am excited to teach you the radio aspect of this business. The marriage of these two subjects is perfection. I can tell you I am at a point in my life when I no longer request radio interviews. I have done so many that stations, programs, and interviewers now come to me as an expert in my field to be interviewed on many different media mediums and also in magazines.

Being interviewed in magazines, on television shows, on radio programs, and so forth has a life of its own, and why? Because I chose to become an author, because my books went bestseller, and because they were written about particular subject matters that people are interested in. This is all of what is available to you and I can promise you that your book lays the ground work for your platform to success. It is not the final word; it is actually the start of your conversation; it is a widely accepted credential in a large number of venues.

When we teach you this information, take it and go for it - absolutely go for becoming a bestseller. It is an asset to TV studios, radio shows, speaking events, boardrooms, web pages, blogs, news print, and most importantly, to other people's minds. We all know getting a book published is the start of the journey where you build your name, your brand and your expertise, including your platform.

Your book is your masterpiece; it is time to create it into being a bestseller.

VIKI: I love it. I love your enthusiasm, Debbi; it is so exciting. I want to share that I used to raise show dogs. I did this for a number of years—I am talking thirty-five years ago. I used to say there is nothing that I have experienced like the birth of a puppy because I had the same excitement every time a litter would come. Now I experienced that when we are moving books to bestseller every week and I feel that way about every one of our bestsellers. The authors are ecstatic. It's the same excitement that I felt the very first time I ever experienced doing a best-selling launch. I feel it every single time; it doesn't ever go away. Any birth, be it living or a book, is exciting and unbelievable. I can't even begin to tell you. Being a successful author is something everyone has to do.

DEBBI: Yes, I can understand what you are saying, Viki, and thank you for that fun perspective relating it to when you worked raising show dogs. I think it is an incredible feeling—the birth and beginning of anything—it's why we get so juiced over our bestseller launches. It is completely different every time, working with different authors on their book, each time it is a little bit of a unique process. Although it follows the same basic recipe and formula, things turn out a wee bit different for each author. There is always that element of challenge, of not knowing exactly how it will turn out until you actually get there.

There is so much that goes into a bestseller book launch and it is so worth the journey. I encourage each of you to keep us in the loop on how you are doing in your personal book journeys. I hope you are very excited with what you've already learned. In the next chapter, we will share about radio interviews and what's possible for you in being interviewed on radio: how to do it, how to put together your media package, and most importantly, when you are on air how to be the most exquisite interview guest you can be, how to be relaxed and convey your message in a way that you feel proud.

I am eager that we are going to shift this conversation to the next part of this tremendous author passage into publishing and promotion.

VIKI: This has been a lot of really great information so begin to jot down what you are learning. You can also journal at the back of this book.

DEBBI: As promised, here is a timeline you can use for your bestseller book launch. Some of these are optional to-dos. Many are imperceptive to the success of your launch. This timeline starts the work nine months ahead of the actual book launch date. What follows below will set you up for optimal success.

~9 Month Book Launch Overview~

6-9 Months
~ Create Marketing Plan for your book launch
~ Hopefully, you already have a website/blog, but if not, buy your domain. Set up your site or hire someone to develop it for you.
~ Set up your social media sites and link them all to your website/blog. If you already have these sites set up, be sure to update them, check their links, and upload your book cover as soon as it's available.
~ Create an online Media Kit. This is a place that will have a page for your bio, photo, book covers and purchasing information, sample chapter, video book trailer, a way to contact you, a calendar with your upcoming schedule and events, and blog tour information. Even if you don't have the information for these pages yet, create the pages and set them up so you can add information as it's available.

4-5 Months
~ Schedule book tours. You can either do this yourself or hire a company to do this for you. If you have the funds, I recommend more than one book tour. Determine ahead of time how many books you plan to give away for review

and/or as giveaways on blogs. Be sure to schedule a combination of reviews, interviews, and guest posts so readers aren't bombarded with the same info if they follow multiple blogs on your tour.

~ Determine if you will host a contest campaign with multiple giveaways beyond mere books. You need to know where you will host it, who will help, the goals, and the target audience.

~ If you need to provide books and giveaway items, try to purchase a few each week. Don't wait and try to buy everything all at once. Sometimes bulk isn't the best answer—especially if you're on a tight budget. A little at a time is more affordable when you don't have bulk cash. When I buy things this way, it helps to buy out of my paycheck rather than my book money, allowing me to save it for lean months or for big item purchases.

~ Put out a call for influencers who will read the book and post reviews on their blogs, Amazon, B&N, and other online locations.

2-3 Months

~ Set up book signings. Check local schedules for events and festivals that might be taking place where you can bring your books. Piggyback on their promotion of the event and utilize a location where people will already be gathering.

~ Start posting a few status updates regarding your book launch and what you're working on to start building excitement and anticipation on your social media sites.

~ Start designing and ordering bookmarks, business cards, postcards, magnets, and the promotion items you plan to purchase.

~ Determine budget and schedule for any paid ads.

~ Set up Google Alerts for your author name and the title of your new book.

~ Once your book is listed on Amazon, set up an author page on Amazon Central.

1 Month
~ Fill out questions for blog interviews and return as many as possible. Submit guests' posts where possible.
~ Write press release, including first book launch party dates and times and begin submitting it to local and online media.
~ Post scheduled events on local media calendars, including public community calendars at libraries, chamber of commerce, etc.
~ Send out personal invites to people for book launch party and online blog tours.

2-3 Weeks
~ If you have a regular newsletter, send out a new one or a special announcement regarding your book release and launch party event.
~ Start posting teasers for reviews with links on blog and social media.
~ Continue answering blog interview questions and guest posts.
~ Send out a reminder to influencers.

1 Week
~ Post blog tour information with links on blog and social media.
~ Begin book launch contest and/or blog tour.

Book Release Day
~ Reminder announcement on website/blog and every social media channel with a link where to purchase.
~ First blog tour stop with link and keep up each day until blog tour is over.

After Release
~Prepare your list of *Thank You*s. Thank the people who helped you, who hosted you on their sites, who worked with you to build up your name and your book. Thank Yous go a long way. If you have mailing addresses, send a thank you card. Include a promotional item, small gift, or for certain

people, an autographed copy of your book. Otherwise, send a short and sweet email.

~Contests/Awards—Begin choosing/preparing for contests and awards where you will submit your book for consideration.

~Promote any bestseller lists you make, even if it's your publisher's website list. A bestseller is a bestseller.

~Review conferences and make options that suit your budget and time. Keep an eye on your stock of promotional items for any conferences, any chapter meetings.

~Keep writing. Promotion only goes so far...the best way to keep your readers' trust is to write another wonderful book.

Discover More:
Become a Best-Selling Author and Radio PR Magnet
with Debbi and Viki in a comprehensive class:
BookRadio.Expert

Chapter Five
Your Press and Media Relations
Ace Your PR Skills

DEBBI: We are shifting from becoming a best-selling author to being interviewed on the radio. How do you do that? I'll be sharing the secrets and information to how you are booked on radio, and how you become exquisite while you are on air, all of which are very important because you want to get asked back. You want to be recommended, and you want to present yourself and your book in a really positive light so that your book sells.

Thanks for joining us in this chapter and book of education. I deeply enjoy what we are covering and offering unique information in this way. I don't know anybody else teaching self-published to bestseller books and radio interview media quite like this. The tutelage we're providing includes very important points so you can promote everything you do and be the best at stimulating book sales and being interviewed.

In my experience, it is great to be on radio. I am known on both sides of the microphone. I host a popular, award-winning, syndicated radio show, and I am also a Success and Media Expert interview guest, invited to be featured on multiple programs. I started out as a radio host, and many years later, the program is syndicated on sixty-six stations. I enjoy interviewing people and I have spoken with many authors on my show, which means I've spent a tremendous amount of time reading each interview guest's book before featuring them on *Dare to Dream* radio. I myself have written multiple books and have been interviewed on other networks and programs. And the last point is I become familiar with what authors have written before bringing them on the show. That is much knowledge on several fronts in the book area which bleeds over into the media area. Being an author myself who's interviewed and interviewing authors, I am keenly aware of how they present themselves and the impact their interview skills make.

I wrote my first book and started being invited onto programs as a guest expert. I wrote a second book—both international bestsellers—and more stations, magazine and broadcast hosts wanted to interview me. I initially began the interview merely for book promotion; however, a lovely surprise occurred, and I don't know how to emphasize this enough. It has changed my life in the best possible ways. I didn't have any foreshadowing that writing books and opening the door to appearing on media would ultimately charge my career path and truly opened doors for me to speak on stages and teach classes globally and become known in this niche media field. Although I am still putting out books such as this one, years after my books were released, I am still called to teleseminars to be interviewed and to appear on radio shows, and to share the information and my messages that started in my books on a big platform and to audiences worldwide.

This, too, is available for you. It depends on how far you want to take it and how much you are willing to put into it. When people put some attention and energy on media, that's all it takes to get it started and begin opening doors. The exposure and the breakthrough of what's possible is why we are having this conversation about the next level which is media and specifically about radio. I will address that being quite comfortable as a radio host does not equal being quite comfortable as a radio interview featured guest. It is a whole new set of skills to switch to the other side of the microphone and be the one being interviewed.

From here forward, the emphasis will be on how to get very good and comfortable at being interviewed on radio. The numbers are very positive for those of us on the radio in the

US market, and there is also a positive uptrend happening around the world, too.

Statistics from as far back as 2012 offer the data that weekly online radio audiences reached an estimated fifty-seven million people. Starting in 2001, audiences for radio doubled every five years, and if they were at fifty-seven million people in 2012, do the math and double those numbers many times over for how many listeners are tuning in today! Those are exciting numbers for those of us who desire to be interviewed.

Here is the breakdown: Eighty percent of Internet radio audiences listen from one to three hours a day; forty percent of those people are listening one to two hours per session, that means you are going to have somebody's attention the whole time you are on a program; seventy-three percent of Internet radio listener's changes stations multiple times a day. What does that mean? That means you want to provide a good interview so they do not change stations while you are on the show.

There are so many options and opportunities, and if we are terrific at being interviewed, people will not touch the dial or change the Internet station. But if we talk too much and dominate the show or have extremely long, complicated answers or lose the audience or are boring or nervous, listeners have tons of station options and with a flick of the finger can change the dial to another program they prefer.

An example is if a radio host asks you a question and twenty minutes later you are still answering that question, you will lose people. It is like going to a party and being introduced to someone, asking how they are and twenty minutes later, they are still telling you their life story. We will check out and not want to be around that person again.

Be a really good interview so that the seventy-three percent of listeners don't change the station while you are on. Here is the statistic from Arbitron: Ninety-two percent of the US population listen to radio in an average week. That's really good! News and talk information and talk personalities are still the number one in drive time market.

In 2015, Nielsen ratings wrote: "Of the 243 million Americans (aged 12 or older) using radio each week, 66.6 million of them are Millennials. This far outpaces the size of the weekly Generation X and Boomer radio audiences, with 57.9 million weekly listeners each. The younger generation also listens to a lot! Millennials spend more than 11 hours a week with radio, and nearly three quarters (73%) of their listening occurs while outside the home and close to making purchasing decisions."

Here's more from http://www.diamundialradio.org: "There are over 2.4 billion radio receivers and over 51,000 radio stations worldwide. Even in developing countries, at least 75% of households have access to radio. Between 2006 and 2013, there was a steady increase in online radio revenue worldwide from $278 million to $827 million. This represents an average annual growth rate of 28% per year. The younger generation around the world seems to be moving from traditional radio to online radio according to sources:

"In **India**, a majority of people listen to the radio on mobile devices instead of traditional radio.

"Online radio consumption increased 16% in **Latin America** over the past year.

"In the **United States**, the percentage of 13 to 35 year olds listening to online radio is now equal to that of traditional radio. Traditional radio listenership declined by 2% in this age group in the past year.

"In the **UK**, 75% of 15 to 24 year olds listen to online radio.

In **France**, 20% of women aged 15-34 listen to the radio at work, and 42% of men listen to radio at work. Listened on fixed vs. Mobile: radio is heard daily on devices in listen for fixed and mobile (74%)

"In **France**, 15 to 24 year olds consume the most streaming (59%)."

Amazing statistics. This data is very important to you, your book, and what you desire to create out of your business or life. Why? These figures indicate that when you are interviewed on mainstream or Internet radio or podcasts as a guest, you have access to a global audience you would not have met otherwise. And if you are interviewed many times over, each time it is a new audience of potential readers of your book, buyers of your products, or potential clients. The bottom line is you are receiving free promotion, marketing, and advertising, and when done correctly, you can get quite the results.

The radio show host promotes you to their listenership prior to the show. Many hosts or producers or radio stations promote the interview through announcements on numerous sites across the Internet, and a newsletter. Once you have appeared on the program, generally your interview audio gets archived online for years, and these archives can give you ongoing promotional value.

Many radio hosts also post their shows on iTunes, TuneIn Radio, Roku, Spreaker, SmartTVs, on cell phones, in dash boards of cars, through RSS Feeds, and on various podcast sites. There are so many ways that programs now can be heard and because many of those sources are Internet-based that content is available until the site is taken down, which often means the program will be heard ad infinitum.

When possible **keep your radio show interviews evergreen**, which means try not to put a date stamp on it if possible. Do not use specific dates such as *"January 15th*

2016," because anyone who is listening to your show with a date attached is an expiration date that just occurred. Instead leave your interview a little open-ended, evergreen (if you can), so that when someone pops onto a site and listens to your show, it is brand new to them and they don't know any different.

You also get a lot more time online for an interview. A traditional radio show, meaning a main stream or terrestrial radio show may offer you five to fifteen minutes. I have been interviewed on morning drive time as much as twenty minutes but the norm is five minutes to get your message in.

When you are interviewed on an Internet program, often they make you the primary guest for the hour. In addition, there are online listeners sitting at a computer listening to you so when you say *my website is X* or the host may say your website or the Amazon URL for your book so listeners can go there to buy your book or learn more about you. Since listeners are already at their computers, they can buy your book in real time.

They can purchase your book right away, or if they are in a car listening to main stream radio and are interested, they will need to write down your information for later, which is dangerous while driving! Therefore, have a website that is very easy to remember.

Online radio shows are very positive as there is a plethora of shows and generally they are on once a week and always in need of guests, so opportunities are abundant. You can also become an interview guest for an online teleseminar, a podcast, a radio or Internet radio program. You will need to put together a brief pitch to reach out to radio stations, producers, and hosts, and learn how to professionally introduce yourself.

Over the years I have received a lot of unprofessional methods to attempt to connect with

me and my show. For instance, people will find me on Facebook and send an IM, which is inappropriate for that medium. Facebook is about relationships; it is not a professional work site and somebody will friend me or follow me because they know about my show. I will get a message from a total stranger telling me they just released a new book and want to send it to me, or say one or two amateur lines to get on my show and it is never going to work. I don't have time to deal with an amateur and if they are trying to get on my show in this way, they will not be a professional interview for my program or my listeners. It is not the right method; it is not the right way.

Somebody on LinkedIn wrote to me, "Our second book just came out. We want to come on your show." Then they sent me their website to learn more. This is another improper method, and this just happened the other day. Who has the time to click on a URL and read someone's website? It is not going to happen and it is not the way to do business.

The author's assumption is that they published a book and it is a big deal. Yes, it is a big deal in their world, but not in the world at large, as there is another book published every nanosecond. What's going to distinguish the professional from the amateur? How will you take your book out into the world as a professional who gets recognized?

First to discuss is your pitch. A pitch includes a bio and the first sentence of a bio starts with your name and your title. For instance, here is a bio example. See what it begins with that is clear right from the start: *Debbi Dachinger is the founder of MediaMasteryRadio.com, and has successfully prepared hundreds of media spokespersons. Her clients have included chiropractors, international speakers, best-selling authors, entrepreneurs, CEOs, business women and men, body practitioners, and financial gurus.* The rest of the bio is anything supportive and noteworthy: awards, accolades, unique facts about the person, meaningful educational degrees, that sort of thing. For me as an author, after my first sentence, the next supportive sentences in the bio are: *Debbi is a radio personality, a successful motivational speaker, was an award-winning actress and singer, and a professional voice-over artist. A popular media guest and speaker, Debbi has been interviewed on over 800 radio and TV shows. She was the keynote at the Women's Calgary Red Carpet event; Global Influence Summit, the Business Success Summit, and was invited to present at the prestigious Los Angeles Conscious Life Expo as well as San Francisco's New Living Expo in the Study of Achieving Dreams, along with distinguished speakers including Marianne Williamson. Debbi consults visionary leaders and senior executives in the world's foremost companies to go beyond "obstacles" and limits of their thinking—accelerating results and catapulting spectacular successes. Clients have included corporations, as well as entrepreneurs, managers, students, celebrities and evolutionaries worldwide.* **Awards and Accolades**: *Editor's Pick: Featured Intriguing Creator, Broadcasting Industry Lifetime Achievement Award, and inducted into the Who's Who Hall of Fame for Entertainment. Winner of Successful Achievements from Voices of Women Worldwide, recipient of Heart and Spirit Award from the Evolutionary Business Council.*

You see it is all the awards, the accolades, the education and back up material. Perhaps you can mention notable people or work in a particular company, perhaps mention recognizable events. Also include in your credentials things such as author, expert, consultant or speaker if any of that is true. In a pitch beneath the bio, highlight one to three suggested topics that you can cover during an interview and include a few benefits of your discussion in a bulleted list.

Your pitch letter needs to be an attention grabber, and it's best to mostly convey the information through bullet points. Keep it short and then send to the host, station, or the producer to share who you are and what you will provide for a show, then inquire if they are interested in having you be a guest. I highly recommend that you create connection by saying towards the bottom of the pitch letter that you heard a particular radio program they aired (of course keep it honest, if you write that, do listen) and you enjoy what they are doing, you appreciate the program and know what it is about.

If you have a press release written about you and/or your book and/or your service, include that in the pitch as well. Most pitches these days are emailed so you can have an attached press release. Communicate that you are familiar with the show and feel you would be a great guest who contributes to their audience, and explain why. Let them know you would be honored to be on their program. Build relationships!

Your pitch letter is a warm up with a short bio, bullet points about what you will cover, a press release, topics of interest you can address in an interview, and how to reach you (your email, your website and your telephone number). The people you are writing to are very busy and require the information outlined like that to determine immediate interest and if they reach out in response to book you, things will move forward rather quickly.

Now **your pitch letter has got you scheduled** on a radio show. Before your interview date, I recommend you learn who the audience is for that particular radio show and what medium it is. Is it online? Terrestrial mainstream radio? Podcast? What are the demographics of the audience?

Do the homework ahead of time by looking at who the host has interviewed. Are their guests transformational? Political? Authors? Is their audience a senior crowd or a twenty-something crowd? Find out because you can tailor how your interview goes for each one of these groups. You will want to know when the interview is going to air. Are you pre-taping your interview for broadcast in a month or a week or a day? Make note of it. Or maybe it is a live radio show—that's important as well. How long will the interview last—will you be on for five minutes, ten minutes, twenty or a full hour? If it is a full hour, what is the rhythm of the show?

Listen to a program before you go on. You will get to know the host, you will get to know the program, and your anxiety level will go way down. It is an incredible comfort because you will understand the rhythm and what to expect. Go to their website or their archive site and listen to previously recorded programs and see what they're like. Do they take music breaks; do they have advertisements? Does the program take listeners' calls? Do they desire that you offer listeners a free gift? Can you do a promo for the book? You will learn much by listening ahead of time.

To prepare to be a great guest and create ease for yourself, especially if you are just starting out, do a modicum of homework to be comfortable with the show and the host. If you've been interviewed for many years, at this stage in your game, chances are you can just show up and be spontaneous and respond to whatever is asked of or thrown at you, and you will be okay. If not, don't try to wing it. You will hurt your reputation this way.

As an interview guest, it is good to **have three key messages** and be really clear about what those are. Key messages are compelling and often cause the host to desire to ask more questions. It will give the listeners a way to connect with you and remember you. When you are interviewed, content is king. You want to deliver, and you can deliver key points. For instance, if I am being interviewed about success or achieving goals I want to get my key points on this subject across.

If I am asked a question about successfully accomplishing a dream, I will use key points to answer what it takes to achieve one's dream. Think about yourself and what your book is about, and if you have three key points, you will do well. You never need cover the whole book, and you don't want to. You want to create intrigue so people will desire to buy the book and you also want to give content during an interview. For example, a host may say, "Debbi what are some tips that you can give to listeners about the dreams that they have. Can dreams come true, and if so, how?" If I were to respond by using three key points, I would say, "Absolutely, everyone's dream can come true and here is why. Unlimited success is a choice. Next, people's dreams are achievable if they will put in the effort needed to make it happen, and third, small daily actions will eventually create big giant results." See how I did that? I answered their question with three bullet points: 1) unlimited success, 2) dreams are achievable if you put in some effort, and 3) small daily action steps create great results.

I responded and did not go into a long, lengthy answer. **Keep it short.** There is no reason to go on and on. Using three key points like that generally peaks a radio host's interest and from there, a host can ask anything that they are curious about related to those points. They can ask many different questions, and it provides the guest an opportunity to address their question a bit more at length. With your three key messages, keep it easy for the listeners to follow and make it a central point for them to follow in a memorable way.

As a caveat, you are not always going to speak in sounds bites as there will be times the host will ask you other questions. They may ask you to tell listeners about your book, why was the book important for you to write, and possibly to tell the journey you took in life: how did you get from where you were to where you are now, having written this best-selling book? There may be a good story in there, so if it is a 20-minute or longer interview, include at least one story in your interview.

A story brings the audience in and makes you relatable. Keep your eye on the time so you don't talk on and on. It's okay to respond to a question a bit longer, but never dominate the conversation. Talk to keep everybody's attention and keep the conversation flowing.

Consider **sending the radio host talking points ahead of time.** A talking point is a topic that invites discussion. Specifically for a radio show, you send the host questions, in advance of the interview that you would like to be asked—five talking points should suffice. Most hosts will ask you for the same materials before each interview—they will need a high resolution, good head shot, a small and wonderful bio for you, your website, the title of your book, and maybe a JPG photo of the cover of your book, along with the talking points.

If you are a published author—or plan to be one—you will inevitably be asked to appear on a radio, television, newspaper, magazine, podcast, or Internet radio show to talk about your book. It's critical that you learn to do interviewing well. Assuming you have written a good book, nothing drives sales of the book more than publicity.

Some suggestions for improving your interview skills are: **Prepare thoroughly for the interview.** Before the interview for your book, identify the questions you *might* be asked. Also write down three to four talking points in response to each question. Don't write out the answer verbatim or you run the risk of sounding too canned. Know or put together the relevant talking points, statistics, and illustrations for your interview. I suggest you ad-lib from that.

Next, **remember that the show is not about you.** This is a big mistake many rookie authors make. You are *not* the star of the show. The host is—or more accurately—the audience is. You are there to support them in getting what they want. Your job is to keep them interested in the topic so they don't change the dial. This is vital to the producer keeping his or her advertisers happy.

What might happen because of the radio interview, and what kind of action do you prefer your audience to take after listening to your radio interview? Is there an angle that you are looking for in the radio interview, and what is your deepest intention or your big vision?

If you desire to grow your business or sell your book because of the radio interviews you are engaged in, take into account that an interview is not a sales job because people will change the channel. Ultimately the listeners want to connect with the guest, or learn something new, or be entertained, they desire to receive some content that they wouldn't hear otherwise, and they want to know why your book is unique. When the link to your book or product is given out, it is a soft sale format, very easy, you and your interview can sell more than being salesy. Do ensure at some point in the interview that you **direct listeners on how they can take action.**

Get it cleared with the host: will they bring up the Amazon link or website, or do they prefer that you do it? You might also consider in your talking points to include the question, "Where can we find your book?" Often, each of us has an expertise that is easy for us as we know our subject; however, the listeners out there don't necessarily know our subjects as well. What do you offer that other people don't know? That's how you can decide what type of content to share—give them something they didn't know before or deliver it in a new way.

I also would suggest **when a host asks you a question, stay on topic.** Don't ramble; just answer the question. One thing you can do to help you is to stay very present. When someone asks you a question, repeat the question to lead into your answer.

Let me give you an example, if I am being interviewed and the host says, "Is there an aspect, Debbi, of gratitude to being successful?" I might answer, "There is an aspect of gratitude connected to success, because gratitude, thanks, and appreciation essentially precede every victorious achievement. Let me illustrate how that works ....." You see, I took the question and put it in the beginning to lead into my answer. What that does for someone being interviewed is remind you what the topic is, what was just asked, and keeps you on track. When you repeat the question, you start formulating your answer around that. It's a little trick you can use now and then.

I'm going to veer off here to mention a few things that radio guests can potentially do that radio stations do *not* prefer– it's about knowing this up front so you're never a bad guest. Let's cover those so you know what not to do. I know none of you will do any of these things once you hear about them. I say this since it is worth repeating, please **don't give long answers**. If you sense you are rambling and possibly have lost the host or audience, then trust me, you have. Take a breath and wrap up your sentence, end it and volley the conversation back to the host. If you get booked on radio and by accident start to answer the host's question and find yourself talking on and on and on, be responsible, reel it in, and end what you are saying. Be fair to the host, fair to the program, and fair to the listeners.

The radio host or producer may need to take a listener's call, so keep what you say to a natural rhythm without hijacking the show with talking. There are hosts that may need to cut you off (money is made on radio shows through advertising), so the producer will cut you off mid-sentence and that's *no bueno* if it happens. Keep your answers brief, finish your response with a declarative sentence that ends in a vocal down tick to make it clear to the host you have completed your reply. Then take a breath with a silence so the host can come back in to speak again.

A true story: there was a Washington DC top-rated FM station that offered a coveted five-minute segment during its show for an expert ongoing guest. The guest was a regular on the show who came from a prominent newspaper, and every time the expert answered a question, he went lengthy. Each of his responses was three or more minutes long, when he was supposed to be just giving short tips—in and out including conversation (sound bites) with the show's host. Instead, the radio host asked the question thinking it was going to be back and forth, but the expert took the entire segment for one answer, he went on and on, never stopping, never pausing, never letting the anchor get in a follow-up question, and you can imagine how frustrated the anchor was. Not fulfilling why they had hired him for these spots, they dropped him as a recurring guest. They brought in a new expert who only spoke in sound bites so the show segments worked well. This is a true story. Talking too much lost the expert the radio segment job.

Another poor habit for a guest is to give a very complex answer. Our goal when we are being interviewed is avoid telling the audience everything we know about a topic. Doing that is too complex and means we can't present the material in a way that's easy to understand. It ends up feeling like the guest is speaking a foreign language and the audience gets lots. Remember when Charlie Brown went to school, and while in class, the teacher was speaking, but all Charlie Brown heard was, "*Whap, whap, wah, wah, wah...*" That's what it's like when we start oversharing on a subject.

Those who hear us will tune us out. If a guest can't explain a difficult concept in simple terms, then it is like introducing an audience to an organic chemistry teacher speaking about complex concepts the audience can't wrap their brains around. On the other hand, an awesome guest can actually take a complex concept and make it simpler and interesting so we can follow and comprehend something new.

A brilliant example today is Dr. Oz. That's how Dr. Oz got to be famous. He was a heart surgeon the media fell in love with because he takes medical information and turns it into small sound bites of concepts we can follow and understand. The media found that they could ask Dr. Oz almost any question, and in just a few sentences, he explains it in a way that is fascinating and comprehensive. Now if you can do that, too, you will be incredibly successful.

Another terrible habit to avoid is being boring. **Please don't be boring.** Radio is auditory. We can't see you, so the voice and conversation should be stimulating. Radio requires energy, so avoid being monotone or taking big pauses. If it's boring on radio, the guest will put the listeners to sleep.

To win on radio, be memorable, have energy, have some animation, and capture the attention of the listening audience. All we have is your voice and your message.

Another idea is to **circumvent being an alarmist**. Radio guests who can articulate problems are brilliant, but they need to offer solutions. If you bring up a problem, also offer solutions.

Please **don't leave your humor behind**. This just happened to me the other day. I was interviewing somebody I happen to know, and he has an incredible sense of humor and is hysterically funny in real life. After introducing the listeners to my guest, I built him up and talked about how funny he was, and how we were going to have a great time on air. Honestly, I don't know what happened to this man, as he speaks on huge platforms. All I know is in the radio interview, he couldn't bring his "A" game. He showed up so serious and that's not who he is. Have a sense of humor and occasionally play and use it appropriately. It goes a long way for levity.

You don't have to be a comedian, and you don't have to try to be funny. There may be some moments during an interview when something funny happens. Have a sense of humor and roll with it. It is okay to laugh now and then. It is okay to break things up and be light now and then. It is awkward for a host when a guest refuses to play along, so if there is a joke or something funny said and the guest's response is silence, it's awkward for the host and really uncomfortable for the listeners. You don't want to have inappropriate humor, certainly; rather, bring a sense of humor, and if something comes up and it is a moment of lightness, just play along.

Now that I have covered the things to avoid, **let's see how you can be a phenomenal guest**—after all you already know your subject and who you are. As radio guests, we only have the sounds of our voices and how well we hold the audience's attention. You can utilize pitch, sometimes rate, sometimes articulation. Be aware if you talking too fast or too slow. Speaking rate is so important.

You are going to be doing most of your interviews on a telephone, so pay attention if you are **wearing jewelry** as a man or a woman, or if you have things in your hair or you have bangles on or dangling earrings—your headset will pick up the distracting sound of the *chink, chink* of your jewelry.

As far as enthusiasm goes, know **we can feel you. Listeners can sense if you have a smile,** if you really connect with the host, and the energy of the conversation. That energy is terrific and we can feel it out here.

Deliver your message with confidence. You know more about your story, your book, who you are, where you have been, than anybody else.

If in the beginning of doing radio interviews, you feel kind of nervous and wish you had nerves of steel or are concerned that you may mumble or fumble, I want you to know right now, it is okay if you fumble. It is okay to start exactly where you are and to build up your skills over time by doing more and more interviews. It is okay to be who you are and to realize that as you keep going forward with interviews, you will get better and better.

The good news is that stage fright is not fatal. It is okay to be nervous and do the interview anyway. To stay calm, remember to breathe and fully show up to be present. You can overcome your fear and give an enormously successful interview.

One suggestion that will help you be composed is to be organized and concise. Spend a little time reading over your materials in advance. That way, you are not feeling awkward when the show starts. Instead, you are reminding yourself of how much you already know.

As the host asks a question, don't focus on the fear; instead, focus on the information, focus on what is being asked of you, and breathe before answering the question—just quick enough to formulate the first couple of words. Those words will open the way to the rest of your sentence and where you are going to be headed. If you are still nervous, repeat the question the host asked you and let it lead you into your answer.

Also, remember that you are the expert, so keep your confidence. There is a reason why you are being interviewed. Make sure before you go on air that you have sent everything that they have requested of you—that will also create a lot of ease for you, and send it in a timely manner. Please do not submit your materials later than the due date the radio station gave you. It is tough otherwise to promote you ahead of time and we want to have your materials in advance so we create great promotion.

If the radio host needs **your media package** by a certain date, put it on your calendar, give it to your assistant, your team, and let them know when they need the talking points, the head shot, the bio, your book, whatever it is that they require ahead of time—make sure they have it by then, if not before.

It is okay to be nervous; however, the fact is you really are just having a normal everyday conversation with somebody. Have a cup of soothing tea nearby or a cup of water if you need to sip something on the break and allay your fears by becoming familiar with the show before you go on.

Know **how the interview is going to be used.** Are you the only person being interviewed, or are you one of many? Will the interview be live or will it be taped? Will there be call-in questions from listeners? Are you going to be conversational? Have you thought about the questions and the answers? Can you explain your key points in a concise manner? Something else you might do in the beginning when starting out is to have some notes on an index card nearby.

You will not depend on the index card, nor will you read from it. Rather, it is helpful to have the index card nearby so if you need a reminder, you can glance down and see it and come back and speak.

I recommend that after you are interviewed, you or your assistants **download your interview audio to keep** because you want to put it up in your website under *Media*. Have a specific Media tab on your website so when somebody clicks there, they can learn more through your interviews. It is also impressive for people looking to hire you to see all the media you have been featured in. If preferred, you can edit your radio interview and post the best couple of minutes from the show, or if it's good enough, post the entire radio show. Either one works.

I guarantee that if you listen back to an interview you've been featured on, with an ear of what you did well, what you need to improve on with your interview skills, then you will advance exponentially.

Ask yourself questions when you listen back. Did I communicate my objective? Did I speak mostly in sound bites? Sound bites are basically short sound quotations that can be used as a quote from you. Try to create a sound bite now and then. Listening back, did you feel that you remained calm? Is it clear you listened to the radio host and connected with them? Was there one host or two people co-hosting who asked you questions, and how did you field your answers?

Did you actually answer them or did you go someplace entirely different, on a tangent, and if so, did you bring yourself back on topic? Were you succinct and to the point in your answers? Did you maintain your credibility as an expert and as an author?

As you begin to be interviewed more often, you will find that every show is different; every host, every program is poles apart from the previous interview experience you've had, and definitely every host is entirely diverse. Because of this, each interview experience is fresh and new. Really know your materials so you walk away feeling very good after every radio opportunity. It's sweet when that happens.

Did you find a place to tell a good, relevant story to illustrate your point? Did you mention where listeners can buy your book? Do you feel when you listen back to yourself that you projected a good, positive image of yourself and of your book or do you need a little work there? Those are some of the questions you can ask yourself to build on your skills.

It is noteworthy that every host performs differently, some are better than others, like everything in life, and no matter how good or bad you perceive the radio host to be, stay connected to them. If the host isn't the greatest at their job, you must still bring your "A" game.

If you need help, whether you are new to radio or have a modicum of experience, or have a decade of interviews under your belt, no matter where you are at, if you require assistance to become a professional and savvy interview guest, I offer advanced programs where I coach clients who consult with me for private sessions and gain big results. I see where clients are currently functioning and then coach them to be successful experts. They leave strategy sessions with their entire media package so it is picked up by media outlets to interview them. I then work with clients on their interview skills and presence. People who choose the Concierge Level Private program go out and are rock stars who experience terrific results.

If you feel nervous thinking about going on a radio show, one tool I am offer to help you feel super comfortable by the time you do your interview is rehearse, rehearse, rehearse. Use a recording device, even one on your cell phone or a handheld, and ask a friend, colleague, or a family member to **do a mock interview** with you. Write up your talking points—the five to ten questions you'd like asked during an interview.

Request that your friend have a mock fifteen-minute interview where they ask you questions and you respond as though the interview is on radio and is real. Record it and listen back. Then answer all the questions above to see where you are doing well and where you need improvement. Your skills will improve with each mock interview, provided you listen afterwards. Also, be mindful if you are saying "*ah*" and "*um*" or using the word "so" over and over again. It is a distracting pattern to listen to.

When a radio show interview begins, be prepared for a rapid start, especially on the phone when you are not at the radio station in person, the very beginning is the conversation time when you, the interview guest, are trying to get a feel for the host, and the host is starting to feel you. You don't want to step on each other while speaking, although sometimes that happens anyway.

So in the beginning, after the host has read your bio and introduced you, be patient and connect with the host, and after the first thirty seconds, you guys will be in a nice back and forth flow of conversation.

How do you rock the radio? You do this with passion for your book, by having a great quality telephone headset to do the interviews, and with a great smile. You can sit or stand, have energy, and gesticulate. If the host has great energy, try to match their energy. The point is you don't want to sound flat.

Don't depend on the host. If you are getting towards the end of the interview and the host has forgotten to do it or it doesn't come up, casually bring up where listeners can find out more about you and buy your book. Do it in a lovely way, but make sure you get it in and make sure people know where to buy your book, and the spelling of your last name if it's different.

Radio is a very intimate medium and listeners pay attention to what you say, so your voice, energy, and intention can bring people in. Additionally, a few times during your interview, mention the radio host by name.

Here is an example. If Viki was interviewing me on radio and had just asked me a question, I might reply by saying, "Viki, when you ask that question it reminds that what I enjoy most about your show is that you talk about dreams and I feel that dreams are so important. In fact, there is a chapter in my book dedicated to the idea of dreams. Do you mind if I tell a little story about that, Viki?" You see, I brought in the host's name, created a warm connection, I acknowledged their show, I brought in my book and then I started to tell a story—all within three sentences.

Remember that the host chose you to be interviewed and provided you with a wonderful opportunity to get your message out in to the world. Therefore, **when your interview is over, be courteous, professional, and thankful.** Write to thank them for the show (after all, they just dedicated their program to you and promoting you for free). If you look at advertising prices, you will have gratitude for being featured on someone's program. I have been interviewed for a decade and I still reach out after the show has aired and let the interviewer know much I appreciate them. I really do feel gratitude and you can create relationships with people that way that can go on for years. Relationships also open the door to potentially create new opportunities that might surprise you, so be gracious in return and then cross promote the show to your audience.

Send your interview information out through your social media accounts, your newsletter, email group, and your website—let your followers, friends and colleagues know you are being featured on a show. Mention one fantastic point that gets discussed during the interview, something that will build interest or intrigue so people will listen live or listen to the replay. Magic happens when the radio station or radio host promotes you at the same time as you are promoting them. It creates a viral effect.

So be gracious, be grateful and definitely cross promote. Are there questions about radio interviews and about what you can do to further yourself and your book?

MOCK INTERVIEW:

AUTHOR: Yes, I have a question regarding your comment about the start of introducing a book, so I wanted to get more insight into that. Perhaps you could give an example of specific things on how interviews might be abrupt at the beginning.

DEBBI: Fantastic! Allow me to coach you how the beginning of a show can be.

AUTHOR: Wonderful.

DEBBI: In this coaching, I am going to play the host and you are going to play my guest. I am going to introduce you and then we are going to get started like a regular interview. Here we go.

Welcome to the *Dare to Dream* radio show. This is your host, Debbi Dachinger, and I have a special guest who has written a memoir. Her name is AUTHOR. AUTHOR, I warmly welcome you to the *Dare to Dream* show.

AUTHOR: *(silence....)* Thank you so much, Debbi, it is a pleasure to be here on your show today.

DEBBI: Pleased to have you with me today, AUTHOR. I am looking forward to our conversation on your book, *The Long Journey Home*. You've just released your book, is that right?

AUTHOR: Yes, it is.

DEBBI: AUTHOR why did you write the book? What is your book about?

AUTHOR: Actually, my book is an inspirational, true story, inspired by my six-month visit to the Orient while on a business assignment, and during the course of that visit, I had a life-changing experience, and upon return, I decided to write about my story.

DEBBI: So you are on a business assignment and you had a life-altering experience. How did your six month visit change your life?

AUTHOR: Actually, being in this multi-ethnic, multi-cultural and multi-religious environment, the communal spirit of the passion and the spirit really created a shift in the spirit in terms of how I view life and the meaning of even love, in terms of the way I was embraced by the community and treated not only as a professional person, but on a personal level.

DEBBI: Okay, AUTHOR, we are going to end the mock interview right there. Feedback: first of all, very good job, and second, did you notice how awkward it was in the beginning before we got into the conversational flow with one another?

AUTHOR: Yes.

DEBBI: It just happens sometimes, like I said what I did and I took a breath, and then there was silence going on, and you did not speak so I jumped in again, and that's exactly when you jumped in as well. It is kind of stroppy or abrupt at times. If it happens, forgive yourself; the host will forgive you, too. The idea is the beginning can occasionally be funky.

Ride it out and breathe, connect with the host, connect with their energy and have a synergy. It will happen. On occasion, it occurs right from the get-go and you click. Now and then, since the interview is often on the telephone and you can't see the other person, it can be a wee bit awkward for the first lines in. To create a different result, the more relaxed you are, the easier it is to connect right away and get into a flow.

AUTHOR: That was a perfect example.

DEBBI: Now let's do a mock interview again and this time, let's both pay attention to the silence with an agreement ahead of time that if there is silence and it goes on for a few seconds, *you* are going to come in with your answer, not me. In addition, let's focus on feeling each other and go back and forth in a perfect flow. We are going to play again, and here we go.

Hi, this is Debbi Dachinger, and you are listening to *Dare to Dream* radio. Speaking of dreams, I have an author on the show who has written a book which absolutely was a dream of travel and transformation that she created for herself. AUTHOR, welcome to the *Dare to Dream* show.

AUTHOR: Thank you Debbi, it is a pleasure to be here today.

DEBBI: I really enjoyed reading your book and give you kudos for sharing the story as you did.

AUTHOR: Well, thank you so much. It was a pleasure writing the story and I am really excited about the opportunity to share it with the audience today.

DEBBI: I think the listeners will be interested in your experience as you have had some pivotal moments living out of the country. Your story takes place when you visited the countries of Asia as a professional?

AUTHOR: Oh, yes, Debbi, I actually, while I was on my journey, I served as an honorary consultant at the university in the Orient and actually was at the University of Science in Malaysia, which was the post. And of course, because of the result of that, I had an opportunity to travel extensively in the area to west Malaysia, Vietnam and Saigon along straight to Malacca to indigenous communities and other remote villages in the area.

DEBBI: And as an honorary consultant, what were your functions while you were there?

AUTHOR: Actually, my role was as honorary consultant. I was in the division of industry and community and engagement at the University of Science in Malaysia and my primary assignment was to serve as a writer for a book that was published.

DEBBI: Okay let's end the mock interview there. AUTHOR, let me ask you, what was different and what did you notice in that second interview?

AUTHOR: There was a little better flow this time around. Much less awkward. And with the practice, overall, it was better. For improvement, do you think I took too long in responding?

DEBBI: No, not at all. Your responses were precise and it felt like volleying back and forth, as it should be. We were off to a good start. In the beginning, it is about breathing and trusting, and if there is sometimes silence in the very beginning, it seems like the silence is extensive but the truth is, if you just breathe, the other person will come in. In reality, the silence is only a few seconds, so trust it. Say what you need to say and then release the conversation. This way, we don't talk over one another and it is very clear to each of us when we are done with our sentences.

I thought your answers were a very good length, contained nice information and, especially in the beginning your responses, intrigued me. I was curious to know more about you, where you went, what you did, what countries you experienced, the people you met—we could have easily had a one-hour radio show and conversation.

Give just enough of an answer and you will keep bringing the host in by creating curiosity and from there more questions and curiosity and questions. A good host will be curious when you are a good interview, so that's a nice reflection on you.

I am going to give you coaching advice to watch your *ahs*. You had many *ahs* in each response.

AUTHOR: *Ahh,* got it—those tics you talked about.

DEBBI: That's correct. Avoid saying *ah*, and instead breathe to collect your thoughts. Start paying attention since your message is too wonderful, as is your story. Do not dilute your potency as a speaker with all those *ahs*.

AUTHOR: Thank you those are excellent tips and I really appreciate it.

DEBBI: One more tic to share. Every response you gave started with the word *"Actually."* Is it possible to drop the word *actually*? Just answer the question and trust that you have the words to convey and to connect.

VIKI: I just want to say this whole entire time has been so impressive and experiencing that transformation during the coaching session was awesome. I am so glad that you had that incredible session.

AUTHOR: Thank you. I am so grateful for it and I appreciate all the valuable recommendations and tips. I have taken many notes and I am going to go back over them.

As I talk about my book, I get more passionate and comfortable. I think in the beginning I wanted to move from the abrupt entry into the interview. I wanted to get that flow more easily from the beginning and these two little sessions were really helpful.

DEBBI: A couple more tips to end this coaching session so people get a lot out of this. These are technology tips and they are super important.

When you are being interviewed on television or Skype or on the telephone, remember to **have your phones and call-waiting turned off.**

You do not want your cell phone to suddenly start ringing, or if you are on the computer you don't want Facebook to make a dinging noise or another call to interrupt your phone interview. To set yourself up for the best sound quality, have doors closed, no background noise, no dogs, cats or children in your interview space. **Have a glass of water nearby** or tea, so if you have a dry mouth, there is liquid in the immediate area. That's why television shows always provide their guest with a glass of water on the TV set.

If you have call-waiting on your telephone and you are doing a telephone interview, disengage it during the interview.

Otherwise you are going to hear *beep, beep,* and you don't want that to happen.

For your interview **be on time**. Always be on time. If the show starts at blank o'clock be there five to ten minutes early. This is courteous and at the same time allows you grace time to be calm and relaxed.

Be professional and **take care of any new technology ahead of time.** Learn it in advance. Google Hangouts, Skype, conference lines, physical addresses, anything that might be new, figure it out ahead of time to understand the technology so you are on time and even better, a wee bit early.

Next, **I endorse only the use of a landline for an interview.** Don't use a cell phone as cell phones may cut out, and for radio, cell phones give poor, inconsistent sound quality. We hear it on the recording when it is not a landline. My radio station will not allow any interview guest to call in on a cell phone, period. Besides a landline, I suggest, specifically for radio interviews, to buy a good headset. A good landline and good headset allow your hands to be free and provide a professional sound quality.

The next thing, please **do not use the speaker function on your phone.** It creates a terrible sound quality. Instead speak directly into the phone or the headset. Also, you must have a website. If you are to be interviewed on the radio, people will be interested in you and you need an online site to drive them to. Otherwise, where are they going to go after your interview?

Have a website, and have your Amazon book URL, which stands for Uniform Resource Locator ready. A URL is used to specify addresses on the World Wide Web. Have those things organized so when the host asks, you can point the listeners to your book and offer more information about yourself, and websites are great ways to work for you.

The next chapter in this book also focuses on radio; we will go even deeper. For now, let's do one last quick mock interview. AUTHOR, do you mind if I use you again?

MOCK INTERVIEW:

AUTHOR: Okay.

DEBBI: I am going to ask you three questions and then I will give you feedback. Let's see how far we can get. Are you ready to play?

AUTHOR: Yes.

DEBBI: Welcome, everybody. I'm Debbi Dachinger, excited to offer another installment of *Dare to Dream* radio and grateful for all of you who are with us today. You may have heard about our guest as she was recently seen on television, and her new book is called *The Long Journey Home*. You might be wondering what that journey was. AUTHOR, it's really great to have you here. Welcome.

AUTHOR: Well thank you, Debbi. It is an honor to be here on your show today.

DEBBI: I'm wondering what your journey has been and how your life changed from that journey?

AUTHOR: Actually, the journey was a transformational journey, regarding my trip to the Orient and it really changed my life in learning how to live more consciously and being more present with myself. I learned a lot about the real meaning of love, family and home. It is really a divine message as a result of my trip that has really changed my life.

DEBBI: You received a divine message that changed your life and learned the meaning of love, family and home, all very important subjects. Where did the inspiration come from, AUTHOR, to write this book?

AUTHOR: Well, actually, I went on this life-changing journey after the invitation to travel for professional service of honorary consultant in the division of industry for a university engagement. Actually, it was a life-changing journey, it took a different twist, being around these charitable, loving and embracing people. It was really life-changing for me this multi-cultural, multi-ethnic and multi-religious environment.

DEBBI: Interesting. And based on the impact of your travels and life-changing experience, I am wondering, is there going to be a second book?

AUTHOR: There is. I am working on it now, actually, as a result of the journey upon return to the States. I spent time practicing this whole experience that I had and as a result, I made some changes in my life as a result of the first book. It really captured the essence of the journey so the next book will highlight more of where I went from there as the result of the journey.

DEBBI: I look forward to that because I enjoyed your first book. AUTHOR, since this is the *Dare to Dream* radio show, what is your next dream? What are your future dreams and goals?

AUTHOR: Well, actually, my future dreams and goals—and I am so glad you ask that question Debbi—is to really be a catalyst for conscious living because I think that many people are disillusioned with their lives. They are looking for meaning; they are looking for purpose, and as a result of my life-changing journey, I have become more conscious in my own life. I would love to share my message and hopefully make a difference through the audience of readers and also through the community of transformational authors and people who are interested in making changes in their lives.

DEBBI: That's our segment of *Dare to Dream* today, and I wish AUTHOR the very best.

Okay great thank you for playing, and I want to give you coaching feedback.

Just to wrap this up, I want to give you feedback, AUTHOR, and I want to emphasize that you **listen to your radio replays to learn more as you build your confidence and skills.** AUTHOR, this was even better the third time. You dove right in and did a lot that's right, and you will be a great guest on radio shows.

Where I want you to pay attention and what is getting in the way of you being brilliant is the overuse of *ah,* and the extreme use of the word *actually.* Overused like that, any word will lose its potency, and it becomes a pattern that we start paying attention to rather than the message being conveyed.

Catch yourself, be mindful if you catch yourself about to say *ah,* when you hear it coming up, take a breath instead, gather yourself and use another word as your bridge.

FREQUENTLY ASKED QUESTIONS:

AUTHOR: If I want more help to get really good at interviews, what do you offer?

DEBBI: With a lifetime of being a professional in entertainment and over ten years' experience working with clients with similar concerns, clients achieve remarkable success. My mission and commitment is to show you how to overcome fear and nerves for a successful on-air experience.

One option is to be privately coached to be a confident, radio guest, learn how to be relaxed during interviews, understand methods to get booked immediately on programs, advice for how to get your message across, know how to promote your business, book, product, service and personality successfully, and have all your systems in place so you are a pro. Let radio work FOR YOU, rather than you working so tirelessly hard on your business.

Clients who have gone through this do extremely well and save a lot of money from *not* having to hire a publicist in the inception of their careers as writers.

You can schedule an exclusive Concierge Level Private One Day with me completely focused on YOU, which covers all the critical information and "Industry Insider" strategies you need to promote your expertise and products "on the air," while effortlessly booking free radio and podcast interviews.

This is an in person, private, 8-hour day plus lunch. I have clients located around the world, so if the West Coast is not an option, we do this via Skype sessions.

There are also individual coaching sessions available which I will tailor to the client's particular needs. Clients leave the experience with the ability to engage in a big game in radio and media.

I am more interested in my customer's growth than their credit card. I take each individual from where they are currently operating in media to what is truly possible for them. I have them fill out a form to get started, and I learn much about them before we work together.

VIKI: Yes, Debbi gets exceptional results. Speaking of results, I want to touch on something that you brought up earlier that I think it is really important. An email is really a nice thank you, and a handwritten note is absolutely awesome. If you send a gift, it doesn't have to be great in value, but if there was something that came up in the interview that had something to do with the host that you found out about them, or you find us through some research on the web, that touches me to no end when I receive things like that. I have to say that email "thank-yous" don't happen all the time and regular mail happens very infrequently. Thank you gifts happen very infrequently as well.

But those kind of things, when I do get them, my gosh, don't you feel really impressed with that, Debbi?

DEBBI: Yes, I do. I have had people who have gifted me with more than a thank you note. The gratitude is appreciated and it creates a unique connection. I have received flowers. I received an Amethyst Geode. I have received Starbucks gift cards (which I love since I am not a sugar person, so for me the coffee is terrific), as well as handwritten notes. I even received an Edible gift basket with a thank you balloon. I interviewed a woman who felt so strongly about what we accomplished together on-air that she introduced me to some very influential people I would not would have met otherwise. She took it upon herself to make several direct introductions to some important thought leaders telling them that they must get to know me and my work. Those introductions changed my life, and changed the course of my business.

Gifts come in many different ways, but it is lovely when the energy I put into my guests and their interviews is reflected back.

Whether someone thanks me or not, I am grateful, as most interview guests are amazing—they are professional and I've created a connection. Viki, I concur, a handwritten "thank you" means a lot when a guest takes a moment to acknowledge the radio host.

VIKI: Absolutely. I do this for clients. When we are promoting books to bestseller, we offer books to say "thank you" for everything you do and for our interaction together. I think it really stands out now because when I first got involved in the advertising business, everyone sent stuff—you know, soft copy through mail, and now you hardly ever get it. Everything is through email, so it's a great way to have yourself stand out as a super professional.

DEBBI: Here's another point about books: I have received books upon books from new authors who wanted to be guests on my show. It was a valiant effort, but was not the way to get booked on a radio program. Use the pitch letter; don't spend all that money mailing out books that people don't have the time to read. The radio host will ask for your book if you are scheduled to be on the show, and then they'll read it.

As an established radio show, I am already receiving books from my weekly interview guests, from publishing houses, and from agents. Remember the pitch letter is the way to properly get someone's attention.

For Viki and me, it's our goal that you feel good about what you're starting to discover here and we are going to deliver more in each chapter. We will keep building on the information we are sharing.

Discover More:
Become a Best-Selling Author and Radio PR Magnet
with Debbi and Viki in a comprehensive class:
BookRadio.Expert

Chapter Six
Your Radio Broadcast
Book Yourself Busy on Radio Shows

DEBBI: I hope you are easily digesting the terrific information being delivered on publishing and on getting booked on radio.

We have much ground to cover with the conversation on radio, what happens on radio, and how authors can be booked on radio. Let me predicate this with a warm welcome from me, Debbi Dachinger. I'm known on both sides of the microphone. I am often interviewed as a success and media expert, as well as interviewing celebrities on the red carpet, at live stream events and on air. I intimately know radio from both sides, and they require a completely different set of skills.

It is my pleasure to share this information. As an author, you can get your message out there through the medium of radio, and you can sell a lot more books.

It's important for you as an author to desire to be interviewed on radio, and please understand why radio is essential. You have been seeing throughout this book that five percent is writing, and ninety-five percent is what happens one the book is published.

You may be thinking about five percent ... that it took you a year or more to write this book, and then edit it, and edit it again, and all the amazing things until the birth of your book occurred. Even with all of that work and discipline to create your published book, it is still five percent of the process.

What that means is that the other ninety-five percent is publicity and promotion of your book. Why waste your effort to write a phenomenal book without getting the book out there? The fact is that radio is your friend and that radio hosts, radio stations, and perhaps a production team are getting behind you and your book for free book promotion. A show or a segment is dedicated to YOU! They have aligned to interview you and get your book's message out to their listeners. The radio host, the station, and the production team have built up their own listeners, their own followers, and maybe they have a thousand, maybe ten thousand, maybe they have half a million in their audience present for a radio show that is featuring you.

Sometimes a radio show is syndicated, so your segment is not just heard on one station but on all the other stations as well, around the country or world that also plays their radio show. Think about the enormity of that—it is free advertising.

Let's delve into the essence of this and its central idea to being an author and a best-selling author. Being interviewed on radio is the next step, and it is an important part of the ninety-five percent. In order for you to get into magazines, for you to get into radio, to position yourself on Internet programs, and appear in different venues, you need to reach audiences. When you do all of this, it is fantastic for you.

We learned about mock interviews in a previous chapter and that's a way for you to be "pretend" interviewed at home. Use a recording device to do a mock practice interview and listen back to yourself. With a discerning ear, acknowledge what you like and what requires improvement.

When you meet someone connected to a radio show, remember **you are building relationships**. Treat all communications with the radio personalities professionally. Treat them with care because how you treat everyone leading up to, during, and after your interview can create much positive work for you afterwards. When they think well of you, when they sense that you are professional, when they know that you do a good job on air, that's when they will tell other radio pros about you and mention that they might want to interview you, too.

I want to point out that part of my duties as a radio host was to listen to other radio shows. I make it my homework on my own time. I do that to keep up with what's going on in the world, because there are times when I listen to a guest and I learn from somebody being interviewed and I am so enthralled with what they are sharing I feel I must have them on my show.

Maybe I will learn something from that interview guest. Maybe they have a great broadcast personality, or perhaps it's their message or the product they're talking about is exciting, or something in their interview is incredibly compelling and intriguing. There are people out there who are listening, besides regular listeners, who may want to take you to the next level, like a producer, a radio personality, or a television employee—we never know who's out there hearing us being interviewed.

Now as a radio host, I have had other professionals come to me when they are doing a teleseminar, a telesummit, or a new show and they are looking for specific experts and professionals to interview. I have been asked on multiple occasions to be a reference for folks I think are great interviews and turn them on to other venues. Since many of us are often in the position of recommending interview guests to others, recognize the importance of practicing so you become the best you can be and of being your best on each show and for each opportunity. I keep a list from every year on radio and every guest and it's easy for me to refer to when I'm asked for recommendations. I just go through my list.

From my list of everyone I've interviewed on my show, there are always people I can pick out to endorse. Praise for previous guests is present for a variety of reasons—they could be excellent on air, knowledgeable about their niche and subject, an expert who gives a great interview, or maybe they are fun and they bring humor. Perhaps they bring some depth; maybe they're a great story teller. It can be one thing or several things that cause a commendation. However, there is one non-negotiable: the interview guest must **show up as a professional**, they must be on time, and they must submit their materials on time. It should be an easy experience with them.

You want to be one of those people that somebody who is in that position will recommend to others because you do a good job. Again you never know where that good job you've done is going to lead you.

When you commit to give a radio station your interview media materials by a particular date, ensure you get it to them by that date. Put the deadline on your calendar as a reminder or gather it together right away and send it off. Whatever date they give, you honor that date, be responsible, be efficient, and make sure all your materials are put together professionally. What materials am I referring to? There is a package that all radio people will request which is virtually the same request each time you're interviewed. The good news is that once you have put it together you can send out that package over and over.

The only thing that might change in the future is if you worked any new jobs, acquire new accolades, receive new awards—you will want to include those in a newly revised bio and package. Another thing you'll want to change up now and then are your talking points, which are the questions you'd like to be asked when interviewed. You'll write up between five to ten talking points to submit along with your interview package for each show. If you've been interviewed often for six months you may tire of those same questions and answers. If so, you are ready for new questions, so write up five new talking points so you keep it fresh.

When you are advanced at being interviewed on the radio, refresh your package because it means a refreshed experience for you on the radio.

Here is what you to put together for your radio package or materials:

You want to have a pitch as you will be reaching out to show hosts in the hopes of being interviewed. Especially in the beginning, a radio host who doesn't know you yet will require a pitch. A pitch tells them who you are, what you've done and what you'll bring to their show rather succinctly, and it is usually emailed to the host or to the station or to the radio producer.

A pitch opens the door for a radio professional to offer you a spot on their program and they will respond with an offer of specific dates and times for you to come on the show. Once a date is confirmed, they will then ask you for your package to be submitted.

Your radio materials or package includes a bio. Your bio consists of your name, your title, what you do, and anything noteworthy about you and/or your company, and includes awards and accolades, as well as your website and the ways that listeners or interested parties can contact you. Also your radio materials need to include a good, professional head shot of you, and a JPG of your book. In addition, you want to include the five or ten talking points of the questions you want to be asked. Offer an emergency phone number for the day of the interview, as well.

Make sure your website looks good. If you are going to be on radio, remember that people will reach out to you who are interested in your book or your work, so ensure that you have an updated, decent website which has links to purchase your book. A good website will be interesting to potential buyers, and people you might do business with. Also have a tab called "Media" on your website. When you have been interviewed on radio or television, get copies of those interviews for the Media tab on your website.

Again submit your bio, five questions you would like to be asked in your interview, anything that is noteworthy about you and your company, including awards, tell them your website, your emergency telephone number and your email address so the station and/or the host can promote you. One JPG picture of you that's a good head shot and a JPG photo of your book cover should also be sent when they've requested to receive it. When you call in for a radio show, you are going to be calling in from a landline, not from a cell phone.

Think about when you had a conversation with someone on their cell phone and you had trouble hearing them because they were breaking up, and you are telling them, "Sorry, I didn't catch that. Can you repeat it or call me back when you have good cell reception?" Honestly, I have had conversations with people within my own home and I will go literally from one room to the next, just a few yards away - it just happened yesterday—and the caller told me I was breaking up. This is why we do not forfeit an excellent opportunity such as being interviewed on radio by using an unpredictable instrument such as a cell phone. A landline will give us excellent and consistent sound quality and that is the standard of what is requested and preferred by stations of their guests.

Now picture that you are being interviewed on a radio show, you are live or being recorded, and you've called in on a cell phone and even though you feel like you have the most expensive cell phone, if you do not have great sound quality for the call, it is a missed chance and they will probably not ask you back again. Trust me, the tiny investment that you spend on a landline or add to your satellite or cable package (you can bundle it) is so nominal and will open up the field for you to have tremendous interviews with perfect sound quality, and you are showing up like a professional.

So **who do you pitch** when you are ready to be interviewed? Often, you are going to pitch the talk show producer. Now with a smaller station, it is often directed to the radio show host. So how do you pitch? You will put together a small email pitch to be sent to the radio host or radio producer or radio station. When they are interested in having you on their program, essentially they will introduce you to their audience with hopes that you'll hold their audience captive. Keeping the audience on each program is important so they don't change the channel while they are listening to you, and that's important because advertisers are helping to pay for the radio show, and that's important because it keeps a show on air. Are you going to deliver a good interview that will elevate their show or are you going to bring it down?

The truth is a radio program is really about the host, and even more importantly, it is about the listeners, so you want to bring the best interview in you that you have.

For your pitch letter or email, pitch an appropriate show. For instance, what is it that you stand behind, what's your message, what's your book, who are you?

Would you go on a republican show or a democratic or a political show, would you go on a gardening show, would you go on a transformational show, would you go on the Rush Limbaugh show, or would you go on the Bill Maher show? I am showing you the potential polarization regarding who you are and what your message is, so you want to pitch an appropriate program. For example, if you are pitching an interview for an Amish romance novel, then you would want to look for a radio station that is in a region with Amish residents or a show that has a strong female audience. Make sense?

Radio producers and radio show hosts get sent books all the time. We receive a ton of submissions every week, often from publishers or PR agents, and sometimes independently from authors (which I do not recommend since there is not enough time possibly to go through all these books). We will read the book of the person we have already booked on our show to prepare for the radio interview.

It is not a correct method as an author to write to a radio host on social media and send your website asking them to check it out (they will not), nor to start a chat saying, "Hey, I wrote this book; please read it and support it." (They will not.) Unprofessional efforts will die on the vine. I am sharing this you because it happens. As a total stranger, reaching out through social media to come on a radio show will not be received well. Instead you want to show up like a pro, and I know after reading this information, you will do it correctly so you get noticed and you get invited to the show.

Let's go back to the example I gave you about an author who has written an Amish romance novel. Another way this author could parlay her book into interviews is through a pitch letter which suggests some fun, controversial, compelling conversational topics related to the book in the pitch. For example, with the Amish romance book, suggesting that there is an online dating site for Amish people is a topic that a morning drive time host would have a lot of fun using as a starting point.

Honestly, talk radio hosts don't often have time to read the books of everyone they interview. I know, you have written this amazing book, you took the time and expense to send it in, you submitted your interview materials which includes your book, and feel they should have read it. However, it is true there will be those hosts who read it and those who don't. What is important is not whether or not they read your book, it is important instead to focus on the terrific opportunity to connect to a legion of listeners who otherwise would not know about you and your writing. You have been given the spotlight, whether it is for five minutes or for a full hour, you have been given the chance to connect with their audience.

Don't leave it up to the host to know what to ask you because you might be disappointed in the direction that the interview takes. That's why you have put together five awesome questions, called talking points, to send to the show so the host goes in a direction you prefer.

Now if you have a lot of media interview experience, mention it in your pitch, using clear statements like, *I have been on Canadian BBC television* or *I have been on NBC* or whatever well-known media source you can mention. If you don't have much media experience, don't bring it up until you have been on bigger name shows.

You can also offer to send a few books to give out during the radio show as prizes or giveaways so listeners can call in or answer something, and the first three callers, the host will decide, can receive a free copy of your book.

The host or radio producer will send you a time frame of when they want you on the show, or they can ask your preferred time frame two or three weeks from now. They will give you the schedule when they can book you on the radio show. All shows are different in how advanced their booking is and how full the schedule is, so just work with them and they will get you on air as soon as they can. If you have a book announcement or a press release, copy and paste it along with the suggested talking points in your pitch, under your email signature.

If it is a bigger, well-known radio show, you will pitch the show producer. If it is smaller radio show, you will pitch the radio host. You can always search the information on the Internet to get a contact name for the pitch. Send out a pitch email that's filled with content, remember it's not an advertisement about your services, it's not an ad about your book, and you want to show the host or the producer that the listeners are going to receive something of value from having you on. And, of course, during your interview, you will get to plug your book. Don't worry, you will.

The best guest doesn't sell when they are on radio show, they inform. So when you write out your pitch, get right to the point. You know what they say when someone is a professional speaker? Tell the audience upfront what you are going to be speaking about and then speak about it and then when you wrap it up by telling them what you just told them. It is sort of the same in a pitch letter and it's done in one short paragraph. That's how long you have to write it, just one paragraph or two, so you want to get right to the content.

I will give you a pitch example so you can see what the flow of a good pitch letter is like. Do **get to the point in your pitch right away. Write it in two hundred words or less.** Something I use that has worked well for me in pitch emails is to use bold font to highlight important points in the pitch so the reader's eyes go quickly to what's key. I figure most people have the attention span of an ant, and I say that with great appreciation. I am a radio host and I know how busy I am; I know how much I have to fend through many hundreds of email every day and filter through on a daily basis. If somebody sends me salient inquiry email that gets right to the point it makes my job so much easier. When appropriate, bold any of the important facts. When they're highlighted, the reader can fully comprehend what's going on and can process it quickly.

Email or letter is best; do not call anybody. Connect through email because they don't have much time. Everybody in broadcast is generally short-staffed and people won't have time to listen to a pitch, even if it is five minutes. Email is fine. Make sure you have an email subject line with no spam words because if it has a spam type word, it can easily be automatically sent to spam, or put into a junk folder and never seen.

If you don't hear back from a radio host or a station, **wait a couple of weeks and then resend the request**. Perhaps they didn't see your email. Now on the flipside, you don't want to be a pest, so if you should resend the email once and don't hear back, chances are they are not interested, so just move on to another radio show and somebody else will be interested in you.

To help your pitch go far, pitch yourself a week ahead of time for commercial drive time segments, and pitch two to three weeks in advance for talk shows and interview and Internet programs. Some morning drive time radio shows will even book you the day before. I have had that happen as an author, where I received an unexpected call from a main stream radio station. It was in fact my dream radio show, morning drive time in Los Angeles, 103.5 Coast FM, which is a number one morning station. It was a dream-come-true for my second book. I literally got a call on the day of their preferred date to interview and they asked if I could be featured on their radio station's show in an hour.

You bet! I cleared my calendar since being interviewed on Coast FM was an intention, so naturally I said *yes,* and *yes, where do I call, what do you need from me?* Now I am glad I am telling you this. It's a great example because my media package was already put together, so when they needed my materials right away, it was very simple and quick: I sent the JPG headshot of me, a JPG of the cover of the book, my talking points, my bio, my website, the link to buy the book, my emergency phone number, and awards and accolades I have won to an email address they gave me. I sent it right out as that package was already together. It was a no brainer and it was so relaxed and effortless. Next, I got myself to a landline telephone so I had terrific sound quality.

Previously, I mentioned that becoming a best-selling author will open doors for you that you will like and will surprise you. This is an example of that. I may have had an end-game strategy for myself with my book and the afterlife of my book. After our radio interview, the host, Kristin, informed me that they liked the conversation so much they were going to keep the segment on their global website within a blog for the station. They kept my interview on their very popular website for a year. How awesome is that? So you never know when you do a good job, and how it is going to show up for you on the back end. That's why I highly recommend that you always bring your "A" game.

Now some popular radio shows get booked much in advance, which can easily be three to six months ahead of time. That's great news for a radio show and its host because a lot of people like their show and want to be featured on it so they are booked way in advance. At times, it can be unfortunate if an author comes to the idea of being interviewed on radio late in the game. Perhaps they reach out to potential radio shows too close to their launch date asking, "My book is being launched next week. Can you have me on your radio show?" And the response the procrastinating author will receive from the radio host is, "I can't, I am sorry but that won't fit into my schedule. I have all these other people to honor who booked my show so far ahead."

Basically you will find an amalgam of different timelines, so **be flexible** because as an author being interviewed, you can easily keep filling in the time on your calendar getting tremendous exposure. It all works out and when you receive a confirmation to be interviewed, don't sit on it, respond immediately as radio folks often make offers last minute, so if you wait a couple of days, you may lose the spot. When a radio show offers you potential dates and a time, answer the phone message or the email immediately to book your interview spot right away.

After you **confirm through email** right away, ascertain what date they require your media package, and either get it in the mail or digitally send them what's needed, including, if appropriate, any product samples, your book, and media materials.

The good news is that you will already be a professional after reading this book, and you'll know exactly what to do the day of your radio interview. **Be on time.** They will give you a call in number or tell you when to physically be at the radio station. Please don't be late, don't you dare be late. Thirty seconds in radio is a long time—a lifetime. If you're late, you will miss the interview spot, and risk getting blackballed by that station. Remember we all talk to each other, so it is important to be early and if they request that you're on the line ten minutes early, honor the request, often it is because they will check your sounds quality.

Perhaps the producer is going to call you at this time. It gives you and them a moment to ask and answer any questions, including how to pronounce your name properly. **Be ready.** Have everything in place, your water, your questions, your key points to remember, reading glasses, a quiet room, etc., and turn off your telephone's call-waiting.

Being prepared and early allows time for you to chill out, to get centered, so when they call you (or you call in to the line they give you), you will be ready to connect and have a terrific interview. Remember when the radio interview is done, follow up with a thank you, something handwritten to the radio host is preferred, but at least send an email of gratitude to stay in touch, to let the host know what's happening with your book, and don't let it be a one-sided conversation all about you—when you follow up with a radio host, communicate how fabulous their show was and your appreciation for the terrific opportunity. Also **be interested in them**. Ask them," How are you doing?"

If you should check in with them from time to time, inquire, "How is your amazing show? I happened to listen to your segment on X radio station, and I think you did such a great job." Be interested in them and they will appreciate you for it. It's not necessary to do this with everyone you meet and are interviewed by. There will, however, be those standouts, and if you have time to cultivate media relations, you can actually create a new set of friends or colleagues from that practice.

When I talk about the media kit or the press kit that accompanies your pitch, only send it to the radio producer or host *after* you have been booked on the show. With your pitch email, you're just introducing yourself to them, making it intriguing and compelling, and if they are interested, they will book you on the show. They send back any openings and you will come up with a common date and time that is agreed upon. Next, the producer or host will request what they need from you, and that's when you send out your book, head shot, bio and everything else media-related.

The pitch letter is a teaser that you are newsworthy, it has an angle you can start off that will grab the host's attention, such as How Your Business Can Make History, something that makes your niche and a potential interview with you unique. You can target the rest of the letter to that particular radio station explaining why your book or your story will relate or assist their audience. Keep it short and sweet to entice the reader to look at the rest of your pitch letter.

Your pitch letter is your proposal that shares who you are, why you are a good person to do this show, and gives a sense of your background or passion. You can include any plans you have for using social media and other promotion tools to attract audiences to this radio show should you be interviewed. As radio hosts when we hear you tell us, "I have a reach of ten thousand and I am connected on XYZ social and I am going to put out newsletters and drive a lot of people to your show in our interview," it is golden. That means we will both be **cross promoting** your show, which is magical and it means that you care enough to tell others about the host and their show. It becomes a two-way street.

When the host and the station are doing all the promotional work for you, it's not as powerful as if you have the two of you promoting to different databases and media sites. This practice increases the velocity of positive marketing and promotion, and is much more powerful to get many more listeners attracted to hear your radio show.

The next idea to cover is **how are you at doing interviews?** Do you require one-on-one coaching to become relaxed and much better at it? Are you terrific at interviews? Are you confident or do you need support there? Are your skills great, or is it essential for you to have mentoring on your performance? Do you need on-air training, and are you in need of feedback to help you soar? Every opportunity you have for radio interviews, for getting your book out there is important, and when each break comes along, utilize it for the promotional gift that it is.

If you show up as a professional, the result will be aces. If you experience issues or you say *um* or *ah* a lot, or you stumble over your words, or you find you are nervous, perhaps something is not working for you. The great news is that you can get better—there are techniques and skills to help you improve until you are so amazing at being *you* on-air that you can be exquisite while being interviewed. If you need further training, get it so that when opportunity knocks, you can easily flow with each prospect and create a tsunami of positive press with great ease. Absolutely allow yourself that.

I offer Media Mastery classes that cover everything from how to host your own radio show to how to be booked and do radio interviews brilliantly. The course teaches everything to be fully radio ready. It includes one-on-one, high-level coaching. Media Mastery is done through VIP One-Day where I spend an entire day with one client privately. By the time the VIP day is complete, the client is akin to a rocket ready to fly. The client leaves with the chops and professional skills. All the bugs, poor habits, or problems holding them back are fixed so they can quickly move forward. Media Mastery is also taught through small groups as well as larger workshops. For those needing or desiring more radio mastery, that is available to you after this.

Authors doing book launches need to align themselves for radio interviews. Include it in the timeline for your book launch and make sure it is appropriately timed.

How about your website? Maybe your website needs to be retooled, put together better, or revamped? Add that to your timeline. Make sure that your event launch is well timed so it is less stressful for you, and easy. Your website should have an easy way for folks to get a hold of you (a "Contact" page). Have a page on your site, or create a new landing page specifically for your new book and its launch.

As promised, this is an example of a pitch letter that I wrote and I offer it to you as a **sample pitch note**.

\\

Greetings Gloria,

My name is Debbi Dachinger, and I am the author of *Wisdom to Success: The Surefire Secrets to Accomplish All Your Dreams*. I have reviewed your show archives and believe I would be a great guest for your radio audience.

Proposed Topic: Characteristics of Greatness

Did you know that a recent survey shows that more than ninety percent of Americans would like to make a dream come true, but don't know how?

At the same time, people are looking for instructions on how to make that happen since they experience disappointment and often abandon the idea of their dreams.

In an effort to understand how successful people think and what drives them, I have deciphered what truly thriving people consistently do to succeed at anything they put their minds to.

As a guest on your show, I propose discussing the following key points:
-How can you take 100% responsibility for your life?
-Simple strategies to live your life on purpose.
-Options to make a plan for achieving your goals.
-Methods for building and excitement and propelling your dream to move forward.
-How to create course adjustments when things aren't working.
-Why you must dream big enough to redefine you.

I have years of experience as a radio show guest and I'm an international best-selling author of several books, with an expertise in success. I assure you that our time together on-air will be well spent with focus on delivering value to your audience. I am happy to provide you with sample interview questions and a complimentary copy of my book at your request.

Thank you very much for your consideration. I look forward to hearing back from you.
Warm regards
Debbi Dachinger
my contact information
email
phone
website URL

~~~~~~

At the bottom of your pitch letter include all your contact information: email, cell phone, and website URL.

Again, here are some reminders of what to include in the letter: address it to the host or the producer of the show by name, write a compelling introduction that captures interest, provide a simple list of three to five key discussion points, mention previous interview experience (it increases their confidence and lets them know you will be a great guest) and if you don't have previous interview experience, just assure the host that your goal is to provide an informative interview for his or her audience.

Offer to send them a complimentary copy of the book you have written for review. This helps the producer or host understand what you've written and gives them more reason to talk about your book on-air. Now we know what they are looking for and what they want you to send after you are booked on radio.

A very good site to reference is called Arbitron. Arbitron was bought out by Neilson; if you ever want to know the radio ranking for a particular station go to nielsen.com/us/en/solutions/capabilities/audio.html where you will find radio rankings, market rankings, and national radio services.

Let's talk a little bit about **working with the radio show team** and how important they are. When they give you a due date to submit your materials, be on time even a little early is fine, but always on time. Send your bio, five talking points, your website, telephone number, email address, and anything else to promote on-air, including .jpeg pictures, and your emergency telephone number for the day of the show. I am repeating this information because repetition is our friend and helps information sink in.

Now let's say you are showing up for an interview, whether in person or on the telephone, and you had a rough day, a really tough day. It happens to everybody, so what do you do? You **leave the bad day at the door**. Whatever has been going on before your interview, no matter how legitimate, never bring it to that radio show, that television station, that interview—let it go. Bring only terrific, upbeat energy in with you and do not share your bad day with anyone. For instance, when you get on the telephone with the host or the producer and they say, "Hi, Charles, we are so excited to have you on the show. So how are you today? How is everything going?" Do not go into, "Actually, my car broke down and then this bad thing happened...." *Don't*. Being interviewed on radio is an amazing opportunity. Recognize that it is not their job to ease your emotional distress, nor to bring your energy back up or even to listen to your woes. Rather, take the time to arrive early, breathe deeply, center yourself while you are waiting, choose to release everything, and be focused on your message, and your interview will be a wonderful experience.

The beautiful thing is that 100% of the time you will find that by the end of the interview, you will be altered anyway and in a completely different place than when you started. You often will feel energized, you will be happy, and you will turn your day around.

Do get to know the show that you are going to be interviewed on ahead of time. Listen to one or more of their previous programs with others guests. It is fun and simple preparation homework. I recommend you listen to the program before your engagement on the show.

I have been interviewed for over a decade. When I am booked on a show, sometime *before* the interview date, it is my job to listen to at least one show. It is tremendous as a confidence builder because it preps you heading into the situation because you'll know the vibe of the show, the host's personality, if it is one host or two, if are you on for five minutes or an hour, where the commercial breaks are placed and for how long, whether or not the radio show plays music, and whether or not they invite live callers? Hearing this ahead of time and how the show generally plays out can be a great assist for when it is your turn.

Now if you are advanced at interviews, meaning that you have done many radio interviews already and you feel confident in doing so, then to become even better, look at where your interview experience is becoming stale. **Where**

do you need to refresh and renew? When you are advanced as a radio interview guest, it is helpful from time to time to periodically switch things up. Sometimes the same listeners may hear you on different radio shows, since they may follow you.

That's when it is nice to switch up your talking points and answers so people receive something new and fresh from you. How do you refresh your radio media? Look at your website and see what needs to be updated. Do you have your media interviews up there (potential followers, clients, purchasers will listen and even media people might look at your media section on your website)? Another way to refresh is to pop in five new questions, switch up your approach, and perhaps put together new material for your website.

Your URL is often sent to the various producers. To see what can be invigorated, hone in on what is authentic about you now. You have changed in the past year or two, or three years that you have been doing interviews. Honor who you are now to revive your media package and what you bring to radio shows.

Since you are a totally different person today, **what new stories do you have to tell?** What new information or compelling content would you like to share? These elements are found organically and you'll start becoming more spontaneous as well as ad-libbing the more advanced you are at being interviewed through broadcast. Before you appear on air, do you know the demographics of the audience that you will be speaking to? If you are a beginner at this, keep a little sheet with you with your key points or important data to remember if needed. It can be an index card.

When asked questions during the interview, **don't be married to your responses,** as the host may take you in a whole different direction or you may answer something and get the host's curiosity up and they start asking you spontaneous questions. When you have a little index card next to you, you can glance at key points written out like a few words that will spark your memory. You can ad-lib from there, focusing on what question has been asked of you, and be sure to answer that question.

Now what if your book is written about a tough situation, especially if it is/was a real and difficult experience you lived through? I suggest, if you have a challenging story written about in a book and you're interviewed, don't get wrapped up in anything grim; don't get overly emotional about it while on air. I once had a woman interviewed on my show who runs a domestic violence nonprofit; it is an impressive company that does very good work.

The interview was an amazing opportunity for this woman to get out her message and potentially have listeners support her company by giving donations and becoming aware of this amazing entity. Whenever you are invited to come on a radio show it is a great prospect—how will you show up? How are you going to use the opportunity?

As it turns out, she did not show up at the radio station; she got lost and called the station several times. The truth is she didn't plan to come across town and didn't leave early enough, so she got caught in traffic. Her directions were all over the place, and she was freaking out by the time she called.

She was too late to make it to the station and instead ran into a colleague's nearby office and phoned in. During my on-air conversation with this woman, all was going well. She shared statistics about domestic violence and the people her company helps. It was going terrifically until I asked the CEO of this domestic violence company her background. She began to tell a personal tale of growing up with domestic violence, and as she told the story she became overwhelmed with emotion.

I am not making any commentary on domestic violence; I cannot imagine the horror and the debilitation that level of violence creates. Here is what's vital to this example, this CEO fell to pieces during the interview, crying and so choked up she couldn't talk. For the listening audience, this is massively uncomfortable and ultimately what might have had a lot of impact for the audience to rally behind her company, didn't happen because she didn't get her point or message across. The unresolved feelings that showed up were not appropriate on a syndicated, award-winning radio show; it was not the place to fall apart. She was difficult to listen to and to even understand really, and then there were no sales or support made for her company.

When you have a book or message that contains a difficult personal story learn to be potent in your delivery. **Show up from strength** and we can learn a lot from you. As I like to say: "Make your mess your message!" Instead, this woman could have been powerful by explaining, "This was my history, this is how I got through it, this is how I am giving back today, and this is the success available through my company. This is what happens when people give what the women get and how they get out of domestic violence." Do you see the difference?

I will offer you two more examples of how a tough story can be delivered authentically and brilliantly to create education and connection.

There is a leader, a woman from Sweden with a husband and two daughters. This leader and her husband finished attending a high-level workshop in the U.S. and were travelling back when she unexpectedly got stopped at the airport. Airport security pulled her aside, and after some confusion and chaos, they jailed this woman. She was in jail for four years. They were four awful and amazing years until finally her husband and lawyer were able to prove that she was innocent. The incident was related to her ex-husband and not to her; nonetheless, can you imagine being innocent and losing four years of your life, missing your children growing up, and missing your partner?

This is a real story and she is an amazing, inspirational being. While on-air, she openly shared how she survived by reading metaphysical books, the life-changing courses she took, how she stayed in touch with her daughters and husband, how they fought for her, and what happened the day the courts revealed that she was innocent. She was released back to her family with an apology. In addition, she was completely transformed in jail because she chose a soul journey for deep transformation. This leader uses her life for good; hearing her interviewed is so inspiring and motivating.

Another positive story is of a gentleman I interviewed who runs a business; he is an author and does great work. I happened to have read something about his past while researching him before he came on the show; I was intrigued. Deep into our interview I asked, "I understand you once suffered from a gunshot wound and if you don't mind can I inquire what happened?" Well, he told us a story about a time he managed a company and he arrived to work early, he was the first person there, he opened up and that morning a burglar slipped into the building and when the man I was interviewing discovered the intruder, the criminal held him hostage at gunpoint.

My radio guest has been held from behind by this burglar with a gun to his head when suddenly he heard gunshots being fired. He looked around to see what happened, only to realize that he himself had been shot. Oh my, it was riveting, an amazing story, we were all drawn in. My guest was so eloquent in sharing this life-altering situation. He told us about being in the hospital and what he went through as well as how he healed from it (inside and out).

This is a man who talked of his near-death encounter and the way he shared it caused us to care about him deeply because he was being authentic, and we learned much about his resilience and character in the telling.

There is a fine line while on radio; we all have tales of woe, whether it is about the family we came from or the story we wrote about in our book. If a tough incident has caused us to change our lives and our outlooks, we can share that with the audience and host who are listening. They will absolutely relate, so we can empower and teach. We want to use any story as inspiration rather than cause separation from hearing our real message. Learn to successfully tell your story because guess what? You are going to be asked to tell your story at some point on radio.

Now the last bit about preparing for interviews is to create a document on your computer (or have a physical sheet) that you can refer to as **your checklist** each time you get invited to a show. Once you confirm your appearance put the radio information in the document so you have everything organized on your end.

-What time do you call in?
-When does the show go live or when does the taping begin?
-How long is the interview?
-Are there any music or ad breaks during the program?
-What is the call in information or address?
-Host's name?
-Emergency number?
-When the interview is complete, how do you get an audio copy?
-Most hosts happily send you an audio link or will give you the URL to download your interview.
-If the show aired live, have someone record it for you so you have a copy.
-Preparation ahead of time is a great gift to you, to the listeners and to the best possible program.
-Radio Station Checklist: Stuff to Know & Do *Before* You Go on the Air!

It is estimated that every day, more than 10,200 guests appear on approximately 6,000 radio talk or interview shows across America. In addition, there are about 988 TV shows to consider for interview possibilities. Ninety-four percent of the guests are authors who do not have recognizable names. Radio and television talk shows need interesting guests to attract listeners and viewers. Authors are interesting people. The general public thinks that authors are experts and celebrities.

Why should you be a guest on radio talk shows to promote yourself or service?

-Most radio interviews can be done by telephone, with no travel required.
-Most interviews are live, and allow for Q & A from the listeners.
-With interviews ranging from five to sixty minutes, this forum provides adequate time for you to talk about yourself, book or service.
-A guest can give out a toll-free number, website, or direct listeners to a bookstore to make a purchase.
-Did you know that the average talk radio listener is 35 to 64 years old?
-Economically, talk radio's audience is considered to be among mass media's most affluent.
Relative to other forms of mass media, the talk radio audience is one of the most educated with a notably high percentage of listeners who have attended one or more years of college. Thirty-five percent have graduated with a four-year college degree.

The gap between men and women in the radio audience is narrow. Currently it is 54% male and 46% female.

If you are available to do interviews with the media to promote your book or speaking business, the following checklist will prove helpful. Always remember, while you are there to promote your stuff, you must also provide entertaining content for the radio audience. Talk show hosts will seldom invite you back if you do not first have their audience in mind. In other words, your book will get you on, then you must have something interesting to say that is unique, controversial or fascinating (besides an occasional mention of your book).

Here are a few bits of information that you must get before your interview that will prove to be invaluable during and after the interview:

☑ Date of initial call. Be prepared to follow-up. If you do not receive a call-back after the 2nd call, send a book cover postcard, give them time to receive it and call again.

Schmooze with the receptionist. On one occasion, I was having trouble getting the producer to return my call. After several conversations with the receptionist, we were getting to be good friends. I sent *her* a signed copy of my book and hinted at passing it by the producer. The day after she received it the producer called and booked me as a guest.

If you cannot get a positive response after the 3rd or 4th call, give it up, shout, "Next!" and call someone else.

☑ Producer's name. The producer usually books the show; however you should try to talk to the host if at all possible to get a feel for how the interview will go.
☑ Best time to call the producer if not in?
☑ Radio station call letters, i.e., WOR, KXAM, WLW.
☑ Frequency of the station, i.e., FM 96, 1020 AM, Power 92.
☑ Their complete address
☑ Office phone number
☑ Fax number
☑ Emergency phone number. Keep this handy in case they or you cannot get through on their regular phone line.
☑ This is very important: Will they call *you* or are you expected to call *them?* What phone number? Be sure the

producer has your direct phone number and be sure you know exactly when they will be calling you or if you will be calling them. Generally speaking, the producer will call you.

☑ Host's name. Will there be more than one? Verify spelling and pronunciation. It is also a good idea to have this in front of you during the interview so you can refer to the show and to the host(s) by name. Mentioning the city occasionally is good.

☑ Listen during the commercial breaks for jargon, things that trigger thoughts or anything that will help the listeners relate to you better. Keep a pencil handy to jot down this information.

When I hear a major bookstore commercial, when the interview continues, I will usually say, "I'm happy to know that Barnes & Noble (or whoever) is a sponsor of the Paul Gonzales Show. Your listeners can find my books there."

☑ Type of programming, i.e., music (rock & roll, jazz, easy listening, country) & talk, or only talk radio.

☑ Demographics, e.g., audience mix; 25 to 34, female, etc.

☑ Date of interview

☑ Time of show, i.e., 6:00 a.m. to 10:00 a.m., etc. Your time or their time zone?

☑ Length of interview

☑ EXACT time of the interview. EST, CST, PST, MST, etc.

☑ Be sure to get the host's email address.

☑ Website. Exploring their website can help you to get to know the host(s), format and more. If you really want to impress them, bring up an issue from their city that relates to your topic.

☑ Will there be call-ins? Are you willing to take call-ins? Talk about this in advance.

☑ Ask if it is okay to give your 800 number, website, e-mail, etc. I say it this way, *"It's okay to give my 800 number, isn't it?"* Most will say yes, and *if they forget,* remember to mention it.

☑ Would the host like several books to give away *prior* to or during the show? I often will offer a book or two to give away. I ask them to send me the winner's name, address and phone number by e-mail.

I personally sign the book and mail it to the winner. I make a note of which book they won and add them to my mailing list. When I mail the book, I include information about other books, cassettes, video, seminars, etc.

☑ Would the host like to have a prerecorded promo for use before the show? You can do this on the telephone. Example. . . "Hi, this is Debi Dachinger, author of *Dare to Dream: This Life Counts.* Listen for some stimulating conversation about relationships on the Sam and Kristen Show on KLOS radio this Monday morning at 1 a.m."

Ask if they have a bookstore sponsor that you can call about your appearance on their show. (Name, address, phone number, etc.) Call the bookstore and ask them to order lots of books! If the bookstore knows you will be interviewed on the radio, it is much easier to schedule a signing at their store.

☑ Ask if there are any specific do's and don'ts for their station!

☑ Ask if they will record the interview and send you an audio link. Most will, and if not, set it up to be recorded on your end before you go on air. (Offer to send them a blank CD).

☑ Ask if the show puts links to stories or guests on their Website. Ask for the name of the webmaster, call him/her and ask if you can email contact information related to the story. Go to their site to see the length of the blurbs that are already posted. Email your information to the webmaster and they'll add it to the site. These links often stay up for several months or longer. This also works well for TV appearances.

What to *send* to the Host:

☑ A letter of confirmation (guest proposal or thank you letter). If you are sending a guest proposal letter, be sure to let them know how their listeners will "benefit" from hearing you on their program.

☑ Your bio. One of the most important things you can do is to prepare the interviewer to interview you.

☑ If you have a website, be sure the host knows where to go to get your latest bio and relevant information. It's smart to have a special page especially for talk show hosts.

☑ Send a "thank you" email to the host and include a link to your links page on *your* website that shows that you have posted your appearance on their show on your site.

☑ Copies of your book(s). Most hosts will want to read them (or at least skip-read them) before the show. Be sure to personally sign the book.

☑ Bookmarks with endorsements. (You *do* have bookmarks, don't you?)

☑ Sample questions for the host. This is a list of frequently asked questions or questions you would like to be asked. Some hosts are better than others. Most appreciate having questions to use as "thought starters."

☑ A sheet of paper with your book title(s), 800 number, email address, and website printed in a large font. Receiving this will help them to remember to announce the titles and the 800 number correctly.

☑ Endorsements for your book from celebrities, industry experts, authors who have written similar books, ministers and others.

☑ Endorsements from other talk show hosts. Most people who have been in broadcasting very long know their competition. This is often helpful. Some will inquire about other shows on which you have appeared.

☑ A brief preview of what is in the book(s).

☑ A business card

☑ Your newsletter, brochure, one-pager, news release, newspaper and magazine articles featuring your work or anything else that will help them make a favorable decision to schedule you as a guest.

☑ Follow-up! If you send your stuff to a producer, be sure to follow up with a brief phone call to verify that they received the information.

☑ **Be Prepared.** Have your cheat sheet with your keywords and book(s) in front of you. Be sure to have answers (sound bites) written out for the sample questions you sent the host. Most radio interviews are by telephone. If you go to the studio, take your stuff with you!

☑ **Check Out the Host.** Before appearing on a radio interview, check out the radio station's website. You may be able to view a picture of the host, a bio, and listener information, all of which will help you sound like you're a long-time listener, even though you've never heard the show. If the website features audio streaming, you may be able to listen to the show before your appearance. The more comfortable you sound with the host, their format and their listeners, the better the interview and the more likely you will be invited back.

You can use the Radio Locator to locate all of the radio stations near a U.S. city:
www.radio-locator.com/cgi-bin/locate

Be sure to mention the station's call letters when you are on the air. Also call the host by name several times during the interview. Write it down so you get it right.

The more experience you gain from interviews, the more selective you can become in choosing the stations you would like to be on. In the beginning, I was always ready when anyone called regardless of whether the station was "right" for me.

Remember that the length of an interview has nothing to do with its impact. Whether it's a short or long interview, the host and the audience are accustomed to that format. They *will* get something out of the interview as long as you are prepared.

In sales, it is important to qualify the buyer. I believe it is equally important to find out as much about the station, their format, the hosts, and the music (if any) before you say yes. At first, it may be difficult to say no.

Always send them a "Thank you" for having you on their show, preferably using your book cover as a postcard. This gesture helps you "*stand out*" from all the rest. It has helped me to get repeat interviews; one station. . . five appearances!

FREQUENTLY ASKED QUESTIONS:

AUTHOR: I had my interview last week on Thanksgiving Day.

DEBBI: Terrific, how did it go?

AUTHOR: I felt good about it and I just wanted to get some insights. I know that radio is an opportunity to always learn and do better. I am wondering if you listened to me on radio and if there is any feedback about that?

DEBBI: Well, the first question I have for you is how would I even know to listen to your show? I ask that question with great affection as this is a learning piece for everyone. We have been talking about promotions, we have been talking about sending out links for radio shows and I certainly never received one from you on your interview. If you had sent information out to colleagues, friends and family, I would have known the date of your show, and offered the opportunity to listen to you interviewed on a radio program.

However, I never received a newsletter, a Facebook notice, nor an email. Nothing announcing that you were going to be featured on radio with the direct call letters and website to tune in. I am proud of you for booking a radio program—excellent! And when you ask me or anyone if we tuned in, I ask you, how would we know to do so?

Everybody is going to learn from what you just said. So my first question is: Did you promote your radio interview show?

AUTHOR: Yes, I did with a small circle of people only and I have been getting feedback from it. I specifically reached out to experts who would be good to have feedback from. Also, I agree with you to really get it out there and promote it prior to the show—and after—so that people can be tuned in because for everyone, it was a busy day.

DEBBI: In the future, send radio promotion so we have plenty of time to listen in and plan it into our day. People who treasure you and do business with you will generally support your broadcast interviews when an author is clearly doing everything to get better and excel and is putting themselves out there, putting their book out there, putting her message out there. Also follow through on the promotional end of things, too, or hire a great marketer to do that for you.

My next question to you is: Did you listen to your radio interview replay?

AUTHOR: No, I have not listened to the replay at this point but I plan to and do my own assessment. I know we always have room for improvement. Overall, I felt pretty good about it and want to learn more. I have to do my own homework first by listening back to myself on air.

DEBBI: I strongly suggest that everyone listen back to themselves, especially in the beginning when being on the radio is new. I can personally offer that when I first started being interviewed, I felt at times that I nailed it, and when I listened back, the truth was there was much improvement required. It is good to listen back and acknowledge your wins while you were being interviewed, and any things you felt were challenges.

AUTHOR: I took advantage of your coaching instructions and used certain strategies you mentioned in previous coaching for my appearance on the radio show. I was able to incorporate three messaging points that I desired to highlight, to tell a brief story to draw people in, and to make my overall interview compelling so the audience could be intrigued by what I was presenting. Additionally, I had my website available for listeners and gave homage to the host. I've learned a lot with the lessons in this PR workshop experience. So yes, I incorporated as many strategies as I could from participating in your classes. I always listen to the key points presented in your classes and integrated them into my interview. It felt very successful.

DEBBI: I love what I am hearing. Those are huge wins. Good for you for using what you're learning.

I appreciate you being teachable. All of what's being presented here is a lot of information and the fact that you are taking it out into the world and using these new components in real time is tremendous and will create a lot of wins.

The next question is: What did you feel as the guest or from your perception of how it went, and what did you perceive were the challenges you had as a broadcast interview guest?

AUTHOR: The challenges were about trying to stick to making concise points. I need to have an objective in future interviews to stay on task with my key points so the audience can leave with those points in their mind. I desire to get better at speaking and not getting drawn into excessive dialogue and to give the radio host an opportunity to ask follow-up questions based on what was presented. In summary, my overall challenge is in sticking to concise points and having respect for the air time available.

DEBBI: How much time was your interview?

AUTHOR: Twenty minutes.

DEBBI: It's funny because twenty minutes is a big number and then you get on air and it is actually quick. Make the most of the time you've been allotted. Be mindful; it goes fast. Whether it's five minutes, twenty, or sixty minutes on air, focus on sticking to the point and making the experience worthwhile.

Next, in those twenty minutes did you feel like you went on a bit of tangent with what you were saying?

AUTHOR: I definitely need to be conscious that I stick to my key points and not get lost on a tangent or additional discussions. Just stick to concise points. I didn't get lost in it because I had a plan; however, I found on a talk or a radio show, the interviewer can really veer off in another direction as you have indicated.

One of the things that you mentioned was to have your key points nearby so that you can go back to those key points if you or the host veers off. These are the things that were so helpful to stay on track.

DEBBI: Yes, having your key points nearby help to visually bring the brain back on the right track. Another thing that you can use from time to time is the technique of repeating the question into an answer. For example, if a radio host were to ask, "I read in your book about a purple coffee cup. Would you tell us the story?'

I might say, "That's a funny story. The purple coffee cup was a ceramic mug that changed my life..." You see? By incorporating the question, I am repeating exactly what the host said and my brain goes precisely to the on point answer.

Also, as you get more advanced, you will start to have a heightened awareness of time. I often have a clock nearby so I know that if we started a radio show at X o'clock, and the interview is only for twenty minutes, I will glance at the clock once or twice during that time. It can be very helpful for a reality check. Or you can choose to allow the ping pong conversation back and forth between you and the host to flow—just get the important information and points in early.

AUTHOR: One of the points I learned here is to leave the audience with a key phase or something that they will remember. I thought that was a nice technique as well. Something that they would remember that would encourage them to read the book or to purchase it.

DEBBI: Exactly, an important idea—why do authors go on a radio show anyway? We find a time to say the name of our book and where to purchase the book, otherwise it's a lost moment and the host may not bring it up. Find an appropriate time to make sure listeners know exactly where to go when they want your book.

My next and last question to you is: How did it feel between you and the host? Was there any follow up after the show to the host from you, was there follow up with you and the station?

AUTHOR: Yes, we talked for a little while after the interview. I got her feedback on how the interview went; we then followed up about some further opportunities, so it was positive. Prior to being interviewed on her show, as you indicated, I tuned in four times to listen and get to know her show. Last, I called in to the radio's telephone line quite early to get myself settled and when the host came on, we had a chance to connect before the show began; that was very helpful.

DEBBI: Did you remember to send her a thank you?

AUTHOR: Yes, I did. I followed up with an email and a follow up card in the mail, with a Starbucks gift certificate for coffee.

DEBBI: Ding, ding, ding. That's fantastic. I am proud of you, well done. And now you have another radio interview lined up?

AUTHOR: Yes. I booked an interview for a longer period of time so the rhythm and the flow will be different in this new broadcast venue.

DEBBI: Full steam ahead.

AUTHOR: Thank you very much. This is very valuable to me. I appreciate your coaching and also the opportunity for learning from your expertise.

DEBBI: Every time I work with people, and I have done tons of private sessions, it is gratifying to witness people go from being a nervous Nelly on air to becoming the best interview guests. I've had clients who are quite good and there's something unique about being a consultant and seeing a client really apply new ideas and excel at being phenomenal on air.

I thank you for being one of those who applies what you're learning and for being so hungry to grow.

Here is a summarization and a couple of ideas. If you have a website, see if it's time to update it. One suggestion is to pick out a couple of professionals who do the same kind of work you do, who you admire and are excelling professionally. Look at their website. What about their website works for them?

Don't imitate anything, do emulate the ideas you see working well there. Create a website that follows what will have the best impact—colors? The layout? Is it simple to read and navigate? Replicate good ideas into your website that will give you the architecture to support your business. Your technical team can develop a unique website for you.

In summary, regarding your radio interviews: make sure your message is clear. The purpose of your interviews is to communicate some key messages. You will never get all of your messages out in any interview, nor should you desire that. Just hone in on three to five important messages, identify a couple of main points to link to the audience. Stay on topic during the interview. Come up with some examples that illustrate responses. Have one great story. And always be polite during your interview; there is no reason to interrupt the host or a caller; there is no reason to argue with anyone. Be professional. Even if maybe the interviewer says something that you disagree with, you can just have a nice way to share your own interesting point of view. No need to correct anyone, even if it is in your area of expertise, you can politely put it back on track.

Remember to turn off your telephone's call waiting and minimize background noise.

Basically radio is a dance; radio is an amazing opportunity; and radio is everything that we have been hoping for to put our books out there; to sell our books. Radio is an avenue that when coupled with having written our book, opens doors to new prospects. Perhaps you desire to start speaking from the stage, start a new business or maybe you want to begin coaching and many, many more possibilities.

I welcome that you share your challenges and I welcome you to share your questions. I certainly welcome you to share any wins and how your books and radio interviews are shifting positively and changing.

Discover More:
Become a Best-Selling Author and Radio PR Magnet
with Debbi and Viki in a comprehensive class:
BookRadio.Expert

Chapter Seven
Your Interviews
Professional Secrets to Lucrative Interviews

I'm Debbi Dachinger. Welcome to this chapter where Viki Winterton and I, your two experts, will guide you on how to become a best-selling author and how to parlay that into becoming a PR pro, and have a promotional media heaven.

How do you let people know about this great accomplishment of your book becoming a bestseller? You do that through radio interviews. Thus far, this is an extraordinary book, I am so glad you joined us to be a part of this. I hope you will stay in touch with us as you go forward on your author and interviewing journey. Anytime you experience a win because of what you learned here, let us know. We're interested in what's going on in your world and how you are using the knowledge you're learning here.

This is like a radio boot camp and there are so many components on how to get booked on radio and how to be exquisite while you are on air.

I'm going to **review some of what you've learned,** as repetition brings to light anything you missed the first time and causes the mind to grab on to important facts. Once you have been placed on the radio, follow good protocol to create a great broadcast experience. Remember, after the program is over, write a thank you note to the host.

Get a copy of the interview audio and place it on your website under "Media." Either upload the full interview or edit the audio into a small clip that has the most interesting portion of your conversation.

Send out radio promoting copy to people who are in your tribe, people who are in your database, people you work with, your colleagues, your friends, your family, and potential clients who have been inquiring about your work. Let people know where you are appearing—what time, what date, what channel to tune in to, and the subject you'll be discussing on air. Most people like to tune in and support you. Be sure to announce your radio interview to all your social and professional media in your newsletter and in your email. Sometimes you'll end up booking your next radio appearance on another show from all the positive promotion!

We've also been talking about your pitch and how important it is to keep your pitch letter or email to the radio show short, to the point, and professional. Having a killer pitch can make the difference between being invited on the show or not being invited on the show. You will email that pitch to the producers or to the host and then follow up with the contact to schedule yourself as a guest. We never want to be a pest, but you do resend if you don't hear back in a few weeks. The follow-up message should be something like, *'Hello, I submitted myself as an interview guest for your radio show two weeks ago. I'm checking back in.'* If they invite you on the show and an interview is scheduled, terrific, and if they are not interested or do not respond, let it go and move on.

After you schedule an interview, put the interview date on your computer or have a sheet that you fill out, or place the details in your calendar with all of the important information about the interview. Include the details on that particular radio show, which day and the time it is going to take place, call in number, host name, and length of show. Also include on your sheet whether you will call the station, or will the producer initiate the interview by calling you. Know an emergency contact number.

Some radio shows have a theme, and oftentimes they will ask you for the theme (topic) of your interview and they generally prefer that in three or four words. This is what you will be talking about while you're interviewed, and most stations will use that topic to promote you.

Know the length of your interview, identify when the interview materials are due to the radio station or show. Have a sheet or calendaring system going on for every single radio interview. When you are a best-selling author and you book multiple interviews, it can become blurry. So, to be able to pull up a sheet that distinguishes all this information is calming, easy, and really helps you to focus and align your content to properly show up for each program and be an excellent guest.

You will be providing talking points for almost all shows you appear on. Understand that sometimes the host will not use any of your talking points and may have a spontaneous conversation instead. These interviews are a lot of fun and will really build your interviewing chops. When that happens, flow with it. You're an expert; you know your material better than anyone else, forget the talking points and have a great time being authentic with the radio host in conversation.

If the host mentions that you did a great job and they'd like to have you back on their program, this is terrific news. Put a reminder to yourself on your calendar and reach out to them after six months, mention that it was a delight to engage with them and be featured on their program, and that you'd like to be on their show again at the host's earliest convenience.

As radio guests, we don't pitch our company, we don't pitch our products, we don't pitch our services. Radio shows aren't interested in a show of free advertising, and that is not what an interview is about. Radio is interested in entertaining their listeners, educating their audience, or solving a problem or an issue that is related to your business product or your book. Here are a couple of examples on how to navigate this.

Let's say that you are an attorney who helps clients resolve problems with debt collectors, and there has been a change in the law affecting how collectors can collect debt. You are booked on radio and rather than making your pitch about your firm, you can pitch yourself as a legal expert who can help teach consumers about what the change in the law is likely to mean to them and what their legal rights are when debt collectors contact them.

As another example, you are the author of a new book on the origins of domestic terrorism. You don't pitch the book about domestic terrorism itself during the interview; instead, offer yourself as an expert on why some Americans become terrorists here at home, where they get their training, their goals, etc. You see? It's problem-solution: explain the problem and share the solution. As an expert, that's what it is all about.

How specifically do authors know **what is the right radio show?** There are a gazillion radio shows out there—how do you discern what you are right for? We do not want to align our message on a show with a theme, with a host, with an audience that has nothing to do with our message and the kind of people who would read our book. It would be a waste of time for everybody. Now there is one exception to this— sometimes positive debate can work very well, like a Howard Stern type of show, which can be interesting. Outside of that, be clear about which show you are getting on for smooth sailing.

Several ways are available for you to find radio shows that you are right for. First of all, Google specific words like "your subject, radio shows." For instance, I might Google "goal achievement, radio shows." Maybe your expertise is in gardening, so search "gardening, radio shows." if your niche is politics, Google "politics, radio shows," or "author, book, radio shows." Google may provide a substantial list for you to read through. It's best not to submit yourself to just any show. It's preferable to align yourself with a popular show with a large audience (a minimum of one thousand listeners is desirable) who will resonate with your subject and message. You can look up website numbers of web-based Internet shows by going to Alexa.com. Just type in the URL for the Internet radio show, and read what the actual hits or clicks are for that show. Alexa provides actionable analytics for websites.

Next, register yourself on websites to receive either daily or weekly emails with details from large media sources that are seeking guests and experts. In return for free sign ups, you will receive in your in-box media requests directly related to TV, magazines, and radio interview spots.

The first website is www.PitchRate.com, a free tool which connects journalists looking for sources with experts looking for interviews. The next website is HARO which stands for Help a Reporter Out. Go to www.helpareporter.com. HARO was founded in 2008 and has about fifty thousand reporters and bloggers, well over one hundred thousand news resources and thousands of businesses looking for people to tell their stories, promote their brands, and sell products.

Since their inception, HARO has published one hundred thousand journalist-facilitated stories, over eight million media pitches, and marketed and promoted well over three thousand brands, media businesses, and consumers. HARO is entirely made up of sources of reporters and is a vital social networking resource for reporters and advertisers.

The next one is called Reporter Connection. Now ReporterConnection.com is a free daily email service. It connects busy journalists with experts available for media interviews, and was established in 1985. These venues are extremely legit and set up so you don't have to go searching for the radio shows, they will be coming to you.

Reporter Connection looks for authors, experts, entrepreneurs, nonprofit organizations, and public relations professionals, and helps them to score media coverage.

The next one is Radio Guest List, another free email service. They book show bookers and producers for submitting guest requests. If you are a radio show booker, a podcaster, a talk radio show host or a television producer looking for an interview guest, you'd go there to submit your talk show guest request. The site then emails guest experts and PR firms so that the right show can connect with a guest request. That website is www.radioguestlist.com.

I want to be clear that many people sign up on these sites as well as publicists and PR firms, which means there is competition out there for the spots that are sent out. When a radio show submits a query for a guest, there may be many guests and firms submitting a substantial amount of people. If something pops up into your email from a site that you registered yourself on, for example reporterconnection.com or radioguestlist.com or helpareporter.com or pitchrate.com, respond right away.

If you answer later, it may not work in your favor. To assure that you are at the top of the list, get your name and information over to the requestors. Perhaps they are getting hundreds or even thousands of submissions; there is going to be a cutoff based on saturation points. You want your information to be right up at the commencement of someone's project or taping. Since you already will have your compelling pitch put together and your head shot, you are equipped to send materials quickly.

Remember you are an expert; you are a pro. Read what they are looking for, tailor it to their request, and mention why you would be a great guest for their show. For authors and experts, check out AuthorsAndExperts.com which is comprised of members of media organizations who need guest speakers or need an expert witness, or those who are authors or experts. There are media options there such as eWomenNetwork, Cyber Communications, ShowTime Worldwide; radio networks like Boston Globe, Citadel Broadcasting, Clear Channel Broadcasting, Collectors Channel, BeautyBuzz.com, Today In America, Wealth Management, African American Authors, Expo Your Money Radio Program, Entrepreneurial Moment Radio Show, Our History Project, Business Trade Association, Jewish Journal—I could keep going, but you get the idea. It is a large site with many options.

As worldwide authors, we want to start to know where lists of radio stations are and which we might best fit with. When you reach out to any radio station, be professional in all your undertakings and nurture all the relationships that you develop with people on the radio.

I want to take a pause here to invite you to consider that you capitalize on having written a best-selling book. Once you become a best-selling author and start to do interviews, it doesn't take much, and what happens through your book promotion is you start to be invited to do things, professional doors open, and you're invited to professional workshops, to speak, and to travel, and it is such a wonderful surprise. You'll end up in places you couldn't have anticipated, and it is a joyous ride.

FREQUENTLY ASKED QUESTIONS:

AUTHOR: I think one of the most important things is the interview skills and I want to know more about improving those skills because as a writer, you are writing and now it is time to step forth and share information from your book and your message. I want to learn more about that as, thus far, what you've been sharing and teaching here has been very helpful.

DEBBI: Being interviewed can be broken down into steps. **Consider having a key message.** When you are developing your key messages, think about boiling down your messages: Start with your big message, and boil it down to five key points. Make sure that your key points are true, concise, memorable, and persuasive. Then you want to **support your messages with examples or with evidence.** It is really about the audience; they are the bottom line, so any message should address what is important to your audience.

If you are new to being interviewed, **rehearse your message** and your key points until eventually they sound very natural coming out of you. In a sense, your key messages become branding for you, so when we are interviewed, we have a goal and it's twofold: the first goal is to meet the reporter's need, whether that's a TV reporter or a main stream radio host.

The second goal is to **deliver your message.** You don't have to be slick, and you don't need to be over prepared. Radio is different than TV. On radio, you deliver differently because it is a different format. Live radio is very conversational, so you typically have more time to make your point. Pre-taped radio is about sound bites and being very concise. Morning drive time shows are fun and high energy, so be ready to match the DJ's same level of energy—have a cup of coffee that morning and make your point early. Always make your point early. No viewer or listener will remember more than two to three key points anyway. You have two to three messages, so get those in right in the beginning of those five minutes you are being interviewed, it goes so fast and all of a sudden, the interview is over.

I am going to give you a real life example about how to do your key messages. Let's say I am being interviewed on air with a radio host and the host says, "Debbi, you are known as a goal achievement expert. What have you learned about extremely successful people? What makes them function as a winner?" To get my key points across, I'd respond by saying: "What separates successful folks from those who do not achieve their goals are these characteristics: One - winners decide, and once they decide on a goal, they are one hundred ten percent committed to creating that goal. Two - winners are resilient. No matter what obstacles come up, winners allow course adjustments. Or, if a failure occurs, winners learn from it and use the lesson to approach the goal from a new and better direction. And three - winners never give up. They never, *ever* give up. Those three things: committed decision, resilience, and persistence always create a winning successful individual."

When we deliver our key points and message so succinctly, often the host may be intrigued by something we have said. Your key points will prompt the host to desire more information. So based on the example I just offered, the host can potentially ask, "Can you talk about Committed Decisions a little more?" Or the host may ask some other point that I have just made. And that's how to get in your key points. For each of you, it is going to be different. Have fun with it; enjoy it! It is going to take you far as an expert, as a speaker and as a leader.

More tips on how to be a great radio guest: **relax and be yourself.** Remember you are booked on a show because of who you are, not who you *think* you are. It's an interview to learn more about the amazing person you really are.

Realize it is called a show for a reason. Some experts and writers try to be so serious when they get on radio that they sometimes pour out all their knowledge at once. Authors and experts need to be entertaining, as well. Interview shows are substantive, but if what you say doesn't also entertain listeners on some level, they are not going to want to stick around and stay tuned in to that channel and show. Remember that all radio listeners have to go on is what they are hearing—the spoken word. Content is consumer driven more than articles, and is different than magazines, websites, and television.

When being interviewed on radio, **think in bites, not in meals**. Serve up your radio content in easy, digestible morsels. Think of speaking about your message in five steps, three habits, or four tips. That's good for the audience and it helps the host guide the show; when you chunk information, it is a great way to assist the host in establishing a nice flow and make your point simple for a listening audience to grasp. Let's say you are going to describe three steps to starting a business. If a radio host were to ask me in an interview how listeners can successfully start a business, I might respond by saying, "Three steps to starting a business: first of all, put together a business plan," and the host might step in at that point to ask a question about step one, or say, "That's terrific, Debbi, put together a business plan, that's step one. Will you tell us about step two?" Can you see how that creates a nice back and forth, ping-pong conversation flow? You are signaling to the host I am going to chunk my information and it creates a beautiful framework for the audience and provides room for the host to create a natural give and take.

Next, **allow for listener familiarity**. Radio listeners go with what is familiar and comfortable, so many listeners tune in because the host has been on the radio for a certain number of years. The host has a familiar voice, so listeners who switch to the station and hear the host might say, "Oh, hey that's Debbi. She is the radio gal who talks about dreams and goals." That listener will likely stick around and find out what I am going to talk about.

Now if I have a great guest on, that is a win-win because the listeners are going to stick around. But if I have a guest on who starts speaking nonstop for extended periods of time, even though that listener loves me and loves my show, they are likely going to turn off the radio or move on to another show. As a radio guest, always offer listeners content.

Content is king. Give listeners at least one thing to chew on, to think about, and to remember you by.

Next, **help the listeners see that the host is smart and insightful.** You can respond to a radio host's questions with statements like, "That's a great question …" or, "Debbi that's an excellent point…" When the host shines, you do, too. You should also say the host's name; they like that. You don't want to say it every single time you engage in an answer; however, you can insert their name when there is a natural flow between you two. The listeners enjoy and resonate with that.

By the way, you can also **show the listeners some love, too**. Say something in reference to listeners, for example, "Debbi, as your listeners know, one of the toughest business startup challenges is creating capital." See how that was handled there? I am speaking to the host, I mentioned her name, and I also included the listeners. I am affirming the listeners' knowledge, thereby letting the audience feel good about themselves while I inform them at the same time.

COACHING

DEBBI: Okay, I am going to pull something up and see if we can get some fun author questions going here. I will play the Radio Host, and AUTHOR, you be the Radio Guest and let's see what happens. "AUTHOR, I welcome you to the Dare to Dream Radio Show. It is so terrific to have you and AUTHOR, I am wondering what is it, exactly, that you are an expert in?"

AUTHOR: Well thank you, Debbi. It is an honor to be on your show today. My expertise is in transformational writing. I would like to inspire the audience of readers through my book and through other inspirational writing opportunities. For example, I wrote an article on the inner world of writers to inspire authors as well as those individuals who are aspiring authors as well.

DEBBI: Can you break down your book for us so we can better understand your transformational writing? Are there key transformational points to your book?

AUTHOR: Well, actually my book is an inspirational true story about my six-month adventure in the Orient while I was on a professional assignment that took an unexpected twist where I really learned a new meaning of love, family, home and peaceful co-existence. Through my work, I was assigned a writing opportunity to write a book in this country. I was actually transformed through the charitable services and volunteerism in the community, and by how universities and communities were uniting to build a better community and sustain projects that would help indigenous communities. So this transformed me as a result of working on my professional assignment and volunteering, as well.

DEBBI: I am curious, in your life and in your travels AUTHOR, who are your heroes? Who is it that you look up to that changed your life?

AUTHOR: Actually, my life has been shaped primarily by this venture in the Orient, at this university of science where I worked. I was really transformed by the spirit of the people in the community who were really helping each other. They were loving, they were sharing, they embraced me fully, and actually, they changed my life and my whole perspective about work and love and community and being embraced in this multi-cultural, multi-ethnic, multi-religious environment. I was really inspired by how modest the living conditions among the people were and how they worked together. So that was really a transformational experience for me and it challenged me in terms of my writing and inspired me in this area of transformation.

DEBBI: Great. Let's end the role playing here. AUTHOR, are you open to coaching?

AUTHOR: Yes, I am.

DEBBI: Beautiful. First, thank you for volunteering I appreciate it. The conversation started out where you acknowledged me, the host, when you said *thank you for having me on your show*. We sort of had a nice breath together and I asked you an opening question. You came back in and gave a synopsis, talked a little bit about your book. Now, when I got to the second question, this was an opportunity for you to have a moment, so when a host asks you a question inquiring about key points (and you will get all sorts of questions)—remember we want key points—three to five key ideas, and also add things like an illustration, include a specific statistic, and somewhere in the interview, add a story, because this is when people start to get really involved with you. The host and listeners get to know you; resonate with you. Understand that when we get on radio, we'll receive different questions. Some may put us on the spot—it is going to happen. People will ask questions like that and it's perfectly fine. My suggestion is to trust the first thing that pops up in your brain. For example, if it is Abraham Lincoln, go with that response, if it is Martin Luther King that pops up, or if Eleanor Roosevelt pops up, or if your third grade teacher, who changed your life because she was the first one who nurtured your gifts pops up, then say that person and why they are your hero. When you trust and go with what presents to you, it is often a powerful moment.

Throughout our mock interview, you kept talking about your life-changing trip in a very generalized way, to the point where we got lost and it went on for quite a bit. What you did was basically say the very same thing in your first response and your second response. You lost a good opportunity. Use every one to five minutes to mention key points, or the five habits, or the four tips, or the three messages—directly answer the question. The key messaging is the place where you can start to weave your wisdom in. On the next question about who your hero is, come back with something specific about a person in your life who changed it and why. Remember to go with the person who comes up first in your mind. Also, remember the tip and trick I taught you—reiterate the question into an answer. That would have been a good time to repeat the host's question.

Repeating now and then also buys you a second, a breath. If a host asks you, "AUTHOR, I am wondering at this point, who are your heroes?" You might say, "Debbi, great question. My hero is....." Doing that buys your mind a moment for a download, and when the download comes off, you have the name of the person and a reason they changed your life. **AUTHOR:** That's amazing because I *did* think of a person and then my mind went off in another direction. I can see now that also a short story would have drawn the audience in, in terms of a really mystical experience that I had that set the tone for me writing the book. I understand your point, thank you.

DEBBI: I hear and acknowledge that you knew the truth instinctively inside after hearing the question, you got an answer, but you disregarded it. Actually, once you download and use the name you receive, you'd then have the story. Follow the magical mystical story that led to your book. If you had trusted that, you'd have gone there and answered the question. It's important to be attentive and listen to what's being said and what's being asked of you. Relax, be yourself, and trust yourself. It will be even better next time.

We can aim to propel the conversation forward. We have a short time on radio, we want to get more information in and take it forward.

On another note, **most successful people have had mentors**. Oprah Winfrey has had active coaches and mentors. Bob Costas, Vin Scully, Warren Buffett—they have all had mentors. They all stated they had mentors who played a pivotal role in their success. It is a question that may come up, so either trust the first name that comes to mind, or have at least one person in mind that has been a life-changer for you.

Being open to the radio coaching is an essential step because when you start getting yourself booked on radio, having a mentor enables you to take the fast track into the radio broadcasting 'guest' industry. Being confident and prepared assists with you being exquisite on air, conveying what you do, and being someone they'd book on the show again.

I suggest you **get to know the show before you go on**. What are the demographics? Who is the audience that you are speaking to? Listen to the program ahead of time to be familiar with its vibe and with the host, and you'll feel relaxed and prepared when you are on, which will allow you to be engaged during the interview.

If you are advanced because you've already been a guest on many radio shows, it is important to **switch things up** periodically. Sometimes the same people are hearing us on several radio shows, so give them something new to hear. We can refresh things like our websites, our talking point questions, our approach, our stories, our key points, perhaps put together new materials to send out, share authentic new stories and information, and play more at being spontaneous while on air.

When you do a radio interview on a telephone, **call in from a land line**, not from a cell phone, because the cell sound quality is inconsistent. Make sure you are in a quiet room. Be clear ahead of time about what time you are supposed to call in.

Always **get an MP3 or an audio link after the interview.** Generally, you download it from an archive site yourself.

Let your database, social network, and your professional media know about the radio program interview you will be featured on. The radio host will be grateful that you **cross-promoted** the radio show.

When you do a great job, the host and/or producer will remember you, and possibly recommend you to other shows. They might ask you back to their show again.

Your website will be set up like a pro, so any media outlet can retrieve your information right away. **In your web menu, have a Press Kit**, which will contain downloadable photos of you, a resume, a press release, a short bio, and a long bio. Different mediums will use different bios. For radio in general, you want to limit your bio to a short paragraph.

Mention your awards and accolades. Have five to ten terrific talking points, questions that a radio host can ask you whose answers demonstrate your expertise. Include any past radio interview audios on your website, and if you've done professional video or professional TV, use those interview clips on your site as well, and mention them in your press kit.

Another suggestion is to **have testimonies on your website**. Get testimonies from clients, as well as TV or radio shows. Make your message clear and be the professional that you are. I am very excited for all of you.

In our final chapter, we will be wrapping up the entire process. Everything from how to take your book from self-published to the bestseller list, and then how you parlay your best-selling book into media interviews and become a PR magnet. We are going to tie the process together with information that you are receiving here. Kudos to you for investing in yourself, as so many authors don't know this material.

At the EIPPY Book Awards that Viki's company puts on annually (an amazing event, by the way), I was asked to speak, and I tailored my presentation to the authors in the audience on how to be amazing while interviewed on radio. I then served on a media panel—there was a publicity gal, a television expert and me representing broadcast radio. I met many people from the audience who came up after the panel segment and were asking questions. They were hungry to learn more. I am sharing this because there are terrific authors out there who write books, get booked on radio—maybe even a lot of radio, and rarely see their businesses grow or their books sell. They know something is missing. What you, dear reader, are learning in this book now is an important chunk of information most authors don't know yet.

Start implementing all of this in layers. You will apply a piece you learned and then add and execute another piece that you learned. Add into your radio interviews and you will start to do very well. As you listen to your interview replays, you will begin to incorporate the next piece and then the next piece.

When I became a best-selling author, positive opportunities started coming to me. I became recognized as an expert—the expert I already was—and it will also happen for you when you become a best-selling author. You'll step further into being the expert that you already are. The world starts to recognize your expertise, so say yes to the openings and breaks. It can change your profession, it can change who you are and how you put yourself out there, and it can offer speaking opportunities and other book-writing chances. My books opened doors for me, and I'm excited about what your books will bring to you. I hope you will sit back one day and think, "This is an amazing life. Look at what has been created and how magical this journey has been."

I am looking forward to our final chapter which is the overview and conclusion where we want to ensure you get this process down and you feel comfortable with it.

Discover More:
*Become a Best-Selling Author and Radio PR Magnet
with Debbi and Viki in a comprehensive class:*
<u>BookRadio.Expert</u>

Chapter Eight
Beyond Your Book
Skyrocket Your Success

This is our final chapter. Viki Winterton here with Debbi Dachinger.

I wrote a book that became an international bestseller called *Beyond Your Book*. The main reason I wrote it is because your book and all the things that come from your book are the foundation and building of your platform. It is a place where you can sit with proud credibility in order to make amazing things happen in your business and in your life.

Debbi and I would like to share a few frequently asked questions that may resolve any lingering uncertainty that could stand in the way of you developing a platform for your brand to become known as THE expert in your arena.

AUTHOR: My first question is, how do you establish or know what the various types of platforms are that you can use for your book to attract audiences?

VIKI: Basically, a platform is the formula for the ways that people can get to know you. I can give you an example of what I do in the publishing business so people can get to know me and my organization. They can join one of our global communities for free, or get to know me as an author with a book on Kindle for as little as $5. Then we offer our print magazines and books from $15 to $30. We offer three different levels of classes to get known as an expert, which include exposure to our list and following, showcases on our radio shows and in our magazines, and having their work printed in anthologies alongside top experts. If they really want to spend time with me one on one in order to hone all of their skills and develop a truly comprehensive project plan or have us publish their book or drive their book to bestseller, the time we spend together and the investment increases.

The reason I am throwing out these price points and these programs to you is to show that getting to know me started with a free membership to my international communities or a $5 book that they can buy on Kindle. They can get to know me and get comfortable with the wisdom and opportunities I have to offer at different levels of participation and access. As they get to know me, many are willing to increase their investment in those opportunities. It is giving them ways to build our relationship.

Often referred to as a funnel (Debbi has one as well), people can come in and get to know us for free or for a very low investment, and then they can move to more comprehensive venues.

Some people come in right away and they want to promote or publish their book and they are ready to go; then we have some people who we have been fostering relationships with for five years, six years, maybe seven years before they come to a point where they feel comfortable enough or the timing is right for them to actually develop a relationship with us at a higher level. But at some point, they have developed a relationship with us at a lower investment level and that's really what the books do—develop a funnel or a platform that takes them through different investment levels in order to get to know you better, tap into your wisdom, and receive increased value from your products and services.

DEBBI: When I started out, I was just street savvy and taught myself everything I could learn in order to do my own book campaign and it worked. I became a bestseller and it was exhausting. It is doable, yes, and it takes up a large amount of time. I learned a lot and I also learned that I wanted my next book to be a much grander experience. I determined what my end strategy for my book was and then set up my platforms to achieve that.

I am all about the ease and grace and freedom that having a team to assist on the bestseller launch can bring, as well as the wealth and health of the afterlife of your book. As authors, we become so focused on just creating a bestseller that we may forget that we must continue to ride the wave of what we have created. Writing a book, making it into a bestseller is a magic carpet ride—magic because it starts to open doors.

But what happens on the other side once you create a bestseller, and if you sit back and rest on your laurels, you lose all the game and energy that you set in motion. Recognize that it is a major door opener, step into to the momentum to make it viral, make it much grander than even the bestseller experience, that's where you get a tremendous number of wins.

As far as platforms go, here is how I explain setting up a platform through a funnel. The marketing funnel is a system that helps track the stages consumers or purchasers travel through to eventually make a buying decision. It also lets you know what your company needs to do to help influence consumers at each stage, such as follow-up telephone calls or sending them positive press reviews.

The funnel stages, from broadest to most narrow, are awareness, consideration, preference, action, loyalty and advocacy. Consumers first become aware of a product or service; contemplate a purchase; come to a stage where they have a preference for a brand, model or a competitor; and then actually make the purchase. Following the purchase, they become loyal to the brand or company, and then refer or advocate the benefits of their purchase to friends and family.

In my business, I have several free items available that bring people in, such as my award-winning, syndicated radio show and interview archives, a free inspirational YouTube channel, and lots of free valuable downloads from my website. Next, I have two best-selling books, which are affordable and low priced. All of these bring people in, start the conversation, let them know my work, and entice them to want more. For those ready for the next level, I teach global classes in media, specifically on how to host your own radio program, how to be interviewed on radio and everything needed to prepare, how to create dreams and turn them into reality, and how to make your self-published book a bestseller. After that, I conduct telesummits with very high-end names and leaders, and offer that to my subscribers and followers.

The next step we introduce clients to is my media workshops, as well as my keynote speeches. The next level up is my big packages, such as my Media Mastery VIP One-Day, where I work with individuals to be radio ready. It includes coaching and is a concierge level experience for my clients who are either new to radio or already on radio and want different results. My clients leave ready to rocket their careers and quickly do just that.

Then one level down if clients want to save a little money and still have a concierge level VIP One-Day, they can gather five people to do the one day together and save money while still having a valuable, transforming experience. So you see how it goes from free to payment, and with each platform, they are receiving more than they actually paid for, which creates a happy, loyal customer, and one who desires more of what I can deliver. Does that make sense?

AUTHOR: Yes, that is really illuminating. I see how I can use this for my work as well. Thank you.

DEBBI: I would like to ask Viki, what are some of your recommendations about the afterlife of someone's book? Can you give us tips about what authors can do after they become a bestseller? After the campaign launches and the party is done—what next?

VIKI: My background is in advertising and let me tell you, you can't even get a color brochure printed for $2. My book cost me $2 wholesale. So we just came back from our annual EIPPY Book Awards and Extravaganza event where Debbi presented. When I do events like that, I do not pack brochures. I bring hundreds of my books and I pass them out to everyone.

I also have bookmarks in my books that have all the information about everything that we do because bookmarks tend to keep longer than business cards. They have my picture on them, they have all of our contact information, so I put a bookmark in each one of the books and I give them to everyone that comes to our booth and who I meet. It is cheaper than a brochure and the credibility is through the roof. Right on the front of that book is the international bestseller symbol showing the book is number one.

I realized that my book, which is one hundred sixty pages, didn't cover all the subject matter as comprehensively as it could have. There is so much more. So we gathered interviews and projects that we have done with various visionaries in the business, which are wonderfully educational, and we developed a *Beyond Your Book* program. The book is twelve chapters; the program is twelve months, and every month we have a mastermind class where people can come in with questions and exchange ideas. The actual class is a self-study where you can study at your leisure and over 1,900 members are now networking, discovering great information and getting tremendous value. So that's one example of what you can do with your book after your bestseller launch.

There is a wonderful woman who wrote a book about her dog and she had it published by a major company. Debbi, you may have had a chance to meet her. Her idea for publishing this book was inspired by the problem in finding "forever homes" for dogs. So the author approached us and we worked with her publisher in order to make her book a bestseller. Originally she was going along trying to sell books here and there, but after her book became a bestseller, she went on to doing book signings at major companies like Barnes and Noble. Then she paired up with pet adoption services. So when she was at bookstores to sign her books, the pet adoption services would be there for people to adopt dogs just outside of the bookstore. This paved her way to develop huge events where she is promoting animal charities all over California to get dogs adopted to "forever homes," which was her whole motivation behind the book.

I cite this as just one example of someone who took a little book about their dog to bestseller. I first thought that this was going to be interesting to see where she goes with it because this is a very personal story about her dog. She took it to a high level that changed the lives of many families and many canines who are now going to find a home—that's just one example.

DEBBI: I think what is important in this story is the fact that when you have an endgame plan, you can create the endgame. I also worked with an author who wrote a terrific book about her dog, and after becoming a bestseller, she is finding incredible opportunities. In fact, her story and the dog's story based on her book is being made into a movie right now. She has left her corporate job because now her livelihood comes from the book and everything that was established after the book. She has a very busy life today and she is doing quite well.

I think it is good to have an endgame to have an idea of where you want the book to eventually lead you. What would you like to create? Of course, that's possible, and then beyond that is possible as well. Authors can step up to play a big game; how big a game are you willing to play?

Here are some more ideas after the book becomes a bestseller. Overall, I recommend that authors think beyond their first book. Don't put every relevant idea you have into your first book. Have more material for each successive book you write.

Before you get to the day of your bestseller launch, much in advance of that, have a game plan. Pre-sell your book to particular venues, drip content, release mini chapters, and sell some orders in advance to create a swell up to the big launch day. Have as many eyes as possible on your book before it goes to launch. Get feedback; ask people and colleagues to review it so you make a great book even greater.

Last, make your book evergreen. Put out timeless information so your book sells year after year after year.

VIKI: Debbi, you are so right. Those are important ideas. What has been very interesting to me is that many times I think I have a big game and it turns out that it is just a small piece of a bigger game. It keeps evolving. Regardless of what your strategies are and regardless of how you approach the future with your dreams, leave it somewhat open-ended. I have often found that what I originally thought was the whole game is just one play in the World Series, a piece of a something so much larger. If I were to form a really stringent type of thinking around that original idea, the other possibilities would not have evolved. I may think I am heading toward "this," and all of a sudden I realize, "No, this must be the stepping stone to a much greater vision."

I think the ability to trust that there may be shifts and changes that really make your game grow even bigger than you ever imagined is critical to your ultimate success.

DEBBI: Outside of media and entertainment, my expertise is in success; it is in creating one's dreams and turning them into reality. I teach classes on that, I have written books about that, and I keynote speak around that. The things being shared here are actually secrets you can use powerfully in your life. There are two elements to creating a dream. As authors, it is a dream to write a book and to turn it into a bestseller; then it is a dream to have a successful book afterlife. The two distinct components that successfully create dreams are always the same.

First, you have a sense of where you are going and an idea (whether it is a picture or a plan or a strategy or a feeling), a sense of the inspiration and the dream. Second is the secret sauce, which is letting go and allowing the universe to play its part. This makes the experience magical. When the universe co-creates, it will surprise us with the enormity of gifts and path changes we could not have known were coming.

When I let go, when I back off, as I allow things to flow to me, it is the recipe for a dream come true. There are two pieces: one is to show up each day with a bit of a plan, and execute your projects or strategies to cause what you desire to happen. And the other is about relaxation and letting go; it's about having fun and enjoying people, nature and animals, and whatever you want to fill your day with. Ultimately, to allow the universe to be involved with your life and your goals means making space and taking breaths in your life because the universe's vision for each of us is so much bigger, limitless, and so doable. If we allow both pieces, in the spirit of a big "yes," the river of life will take you on an amazing experience.

I hope you can hear the potent messages in this summary of our program. So much more is possible than most people conceive.

VIKI: Yes, and I think it comes to full fruition, Debbi, when it is about someone other than just yourself. It is all about service.

I always wanted to create a magazine. I had my own ad agency, and we were doing eight figures. After three years, when I was twenty-five years old, we were acquired, and during that time, I fell in love with Andy Warhol's *Interview* magazine. The biggest names in the arts interviewed people who were unknown with these huge, gorgeous pictures. I thought, "I would love to do a magazine like that about ordinary people who are striving for success and have some important things to say." It took me decades upon decades—so many decades until the magazine happened, and behold that magazine finally came to fruition.

Insights and *PUBLISHED!* magazines became my reality; my vision realized. They opened up so many other opportunities that are realities now. It all happened because I saw that coaches, authors and entrepreneurs did not have a venue where they could go to express themselves and very quickly become noticed.

So we started the magazines and the radio shows and eventually the books because of the fact that we wanted to bring people who were less known together with people who are superstars and household names in a venue where we could create immediate impact. That's how my idea of the magazine evolved, and it did so because I wanted to do it for others. It was a dream I never let go of until it became a reality, and has been the foundation for everything that we have been able to develop, including taking over one thousand authors now to bestseller!

It is incredible when service enters into this equation because I think that you need to want it for yourself as an expression, and when that turns into something you want to contribute to the world, it truly is your unique and special gift, and everything that comes back to you after that is gravy.

DEBBI: That's an amazing story you shared, and I appreciate learning about the magazine dream you made come true, which ultimately is a service for all of us. I am curious, Viki, throughout the years that you have been doing this—being at the helm now of magazines and your various dream businesses, what have you learned that you did not anticipate learning?

VIKI: What I realized was that my ad agency was totally dedicated to being able to have corporations tell their stories, so they could attract the best employees and the best customers. Most of our clients were Fortune 500 companies so it was no small task and that really changed me. I also wanted to run an ad business, be honest in all of our actions with our clients and the audience, and be successful in a business where honesty is not always front and center.

I had been in advertising, and then I moved to consulting and coaching major corporations all over the world for decades, and now publishing. I always felt there was a lack of continuity in what I had been doing with my life and my life experiences until I realized that at the core, there has always been a common thread that has become my purpose. I am a liaison. I am the person who forms a relationship between two people or two organizations for their mutual benefit.

In advertising, I brought those who had products and services together with those who needed them. In consulting, I brought CEOs together with their vision for their companies, and then brought their teams together to create that vision. Now I bring out the stories authors have in their heads, hearts, and souls to the people who need to hear those stories. There is a tremendous continuity in all that I have learned and all that I have done.

Once I was able to define that, it was huge for me. I think that's really important because sometimes we may feel like we are stumbling or lacking direction. I have to say that everything that I have done for all of these decades was absolutely necessary for me to be able to do what I am doing today. There was no wasted time, there was no disconnect; it was all divine planning that I would have all this information and all this experience in order to do what I am able to do today. At times, I just thought, "This is something new. This is something different and disconnected." It really wasn't. It was all one purpose going forward to make wonders happen today for myself, and just as importantly, for others.

DEBBI: All the new pieces entering your life weren't disconnected after all. It was one purpose going forward. That's brilliant. My life has been very much like that and it is interesting hearing your story from the inception of your idea, to how you created the platform and all of what was subsequently manifested as a result, to your mission to have a place for authors, coaches and entrepreneurs who did not have a venue where they could go to express themselves and very quickly become noticed. From that mission, you were brought to each necessary piece for your journey. What a great story.

VIKI: I am sure that everyone reading this realizes, and I know Debbi knows this for sure, we never plan as big as what may really happen for us. We just have no idea how many people our dream is going to touch. When our desire for our self transcends into what it looks like for others, then it becomes unbelievably beautiful.

DEBBI: My experience of having a plan and also receiving what the universe has in store for me has been much like skiing down a mountain, where there are switchbacks. I often had a plan I desired to manifest and found the universe often had a plan even more desirable for me. I was open to taking action for my goals and also to seeing the opportunities that came my way and being open to them, which created so much more. Specifically, I was an actress and singer for most of my young and early adult life. After I got married, I began three years of infertility treatments where I experienced a change of passion towards action in a year where I had booked my biggest acting parts.

Out of that awareness led to cartoon voice-over work. I had an agent at the time who was sending me out on voice-over auditions every day. I noticed that a radio station was looking for a radio host. I had never done radio and thought, "That is a good way to get my voice out there." I got the job at the radio station and two months after hosting a small music show on air, I was offered my own one-hour radio program by the radio station. I knew I wanted to do a radio show to help people realize their dreams and live big; I called it *Dare to Dream*. Thus, my program was born. Over the next eight years, the show moved to three other stations with bigger and bigger listenership, it became an award-winning program and then was syndicated throughout the U.S. and U.K.

I desire to reach even more people with my message and so wrote two best-selling books on how to successfully live your life and manifest your dreams.

I then stepped into being a media consultant when I noticed that authors, coaches, and entrepreneurs did not know how to get booked on radio shows or where the right shows for them were. Many required private coaching so their messaging and time on air became extremely well received and productive.

I was showing clients how to get their messages out in a big way: Media Makeovers for Global Messengers. It was gratifying to help leaders and global change makers clarify and deepen their message to create the future they were dreaming of.

The common question was: Do you know how to articulate out in the world who you are and what you do? Can you say who you are and what you do in a way that causes people to lean in, take your business card, and sign up to work with you? Do you know how to message yourself through media, networking and those you connect with to bring in sustainable clients, followers, sales, and fill up workshops? In helping business people, authors, spiritual teachers, transformational leaders and global messengers, many doors were opened. It has been a surprising and gratifying dream journey.

VIKI: This is so inspiring and exciting. How about you reading this book? Assuming that you have written a good book, nothing drives sales of your book more than publicity. Debbi, can you review your most powerful suggestions for improving radio interviews?

DEBBI: **Have a little index card next to you.** It is good for your memory. In fact, this came up in our last chapter. When I was coaching someone during the mock interview, the interviewee said, "Oops, I kind of got lost. You asked me a question and I went off on a tangent. How can I keep my brain on track?" Being on track is important, so one thing you can do is repeat the radio host's question. I do not advise that you repeat every question, but doing so every now and then will bring you right into the answer. If you have a little index card next to you with bullet points and a few key words, if necessary, you can look down and it will spark your memory and you can adlib from there. Keeping your answers on track is important.

The next thing is remembering that **the radio show or the television show is not about you**. Some rookie authors make that mistake; however, the bottom line is you are not the star of the show, the host is. The host is the star of their show and even more accurately, the audience is the star. You are there to help the radio host and the station get what they want, which is to keep all the listeners interested in the topic so that the listeners don't change the dial. The key is we want to make the producer happy and the producer is happy when they are making their advertisers happy. If advertisers are happy, that's because all the listeners are staying tuned in to listen to the show. If you're a great interview guest, they will stay on the dial to hear more.

The third thing is to **understand in advance each radio show's audience**. You can help the audience get what they desire by looking into demographic and psychographic information. It is a good idea to find out any particulars you can by asking the producer or going online ahead of time and researching it.

I have people come on my radio show or just listen to my program who inquire about the cost of advertising on my program or are interested in sponsoring my show. If you find a program you highly enjoy with a great following and the audience is your niche market, consider advertising on or sponsoring the show for wide range promotion of your business, product, service, or book.

The fourth thing is please **don't expect the interviewer to have read your book.** I know that's the worst thing I could tell you because you've just written something amazing that took much time, energy, and discipline to do. I acknowledge it and I apologize in advance for the radio show hosts and television show hosts who do this, because it will happen. I hear it all the time. Occasionally, you will be on a show and the host will have read your book and it is absolutely a different interview when they're familiar with your work. But here is the deal: if they have not read your book, don't get disappointed and don't embarrass them on air. Instead make the host look good and look smart. Remember you are providing the show with a list of questions to ask in advance. The great news is that nine times out of ten the host is going to ask you the exact questions that you submitted so you will be one step ahead of intimately knowing the answers.

The next point I suggest is **learn to explain what your book is about in a few sentences.** In order to introduce your book in a compelling way in just a few sentences, you should avoid waxing on about your novel. Don't get vague or confusing—remember you are a pro. Instead, you are going to craft an elevator pitch so that you are always ready to explain your book.

Here is the concept: Imagine you get in the elevator at NBC in New York City and you discover that standing next to you in the elevator is the producer for *The Today Show*. There you are in the elevator holding your book, when the producer looks over and says, "I see you have written a book. What's your book about?" You have ten floors to tell this producer what your book is about; ten floors equal about three sentences. Don't we all want to have three sentences to share with the producer so they book us on *The Today Show* or any major show? That's the goal—write out the three sentences, memorize them, and you will have it in your arsenal when you appear on shows and pitch yourself. Also, you can use these sentences during the interview, when the host asks about your book, share those three sentences.

I have also found in social situations that people often introduce me and follow up with, "...and Debbi has written two books." The people I was just introduced to always ask, "What is your book about?" Again, those three sentences come in very handy at parties as well. The three sentences can create intrigue to compel folks to ask more or inquire where they can buy your book. If you keep it succinct, they'll stay with you and be interested. However, if you talk on and on about your book, they will zone out and be disinterested. Test your sentences and memorize them—you'll be happy you did.

The next idea to point out is for the author **to listen carefully during an interview to the host's questions.** Some authors who are new to being interviewed may become anxious and interrupt the host out of nerves. Instead, let the interviewer finish what they are saying or asking. If you are new, now and then affirm the question you've just been asked. For example, repeat the question and then answer it so that you answer the actual question.

The next point is **keep your responses brief and to the point**. There is nothing worse on a radio show than a rambling author who is taking over the show and talking so much we go numb and tune out and turn off. The host may be trying to interject a point, or the host is desiring to bring that plane in for a landing, or perhaps the producer has queued the music for a break but the author keeps right on talking. If the music has started already, then it will air with the music playing right over your voice, which makes the author look silly and unprofessional. Speak in sentences and bites; err on keeping it simple; don't attempt to take over the show by talking too much. Start to bring your voice out and express yourself and your message, and it will be all good.

A good interview is like a ping pong match where the interviewer hits the verbal ball over the net, the author gets into position and hits it back, and then we start the cycle all over again, back and forth and back and forth. To be successful at this, learn to speak in sound bites. I recommend that you are energetic and authentic. The great news is that you are the only person they have aligned to have on the program, so show up with some animation, energy, and be your best self.

Last, **refer the listeners back to your book**; it is the heart of the soft sell. Publicity done softly is good when you point the people back to your book. You don't want to be aggressive and salesy or you are going to turn potential readers and the host off. You also don't want to be too laid back because the publicity can result in sales. Mention the book title, offer a few nuggets or maybe a free sample, and then refer the people to the book for more information.

Here is an example. If I wrote a book about marriage, I could provide seven tips for resolving marital conflicts. Since we don't have time get into all those tips on the radio show, I could let them know there are seven and I am offering the listeners the first two suggestions and then can mention the website where they can get the book. This way, the sharing of the site is intriguing and compelling. Without overshadowing the host, audiences are given the location where the book can be purchased. Remember that writing a book is 5% of the job and the other 95% is embracing your role as the book's chief spokesperson. When you do this well, you create a long and successful writing career.

Don't use a cell phone. Always turn off your call waiting and call in on a landline. Make the call to the station a little bit early and thank the host, thank the host, thank the host afterwards. That's some advanced media and training tips for when you do your radio campaign interviews.

FREQUENTLY ASKED QUESTIONS:

AUTHOR: I know that many people write books. What makes a book a bestseller?

DEBBI: What makes a book a bestseller? There are two things and I am going to tailor this answer specifically to self-published books. A *New York Times* best-selling book is a different conversation and the *New York Times* bestseller campaign takes a lot of the author's money and is a completely different campaign when done correctly.

For all who are self-published authors, it means that we choose a day on the calendar to do a book launch. All the days leading up to the launch require a book to be written, properly edited, have a cover, and have an interior, and be prepared to be published.

On the day of your book launch, the sales are driven up for that one day. Why? Because that's how you create a bestseller, one day of sales, in this case on Amazon, and your title will excel in its ranking. In your particular category, a bestseller is created when your book goes above the top 100 books being sold in that moment on that day, and continues rising in ranking until it hopefully reaches number one book being sold in its category above all other books.

If there are two hundred thousand books in your category on that particular date of your book launch, you will want to rise above the two hundred thousand other books in sales. How that happens is we drive sales that day through people repeatedly buying your book on one day. As your launch day progresses, you will start to see your book ranking number drop and drop and drop and drop and drop. That's what we want. You can click on the link to the category or categories where your book is located and when your book starts to get to the top, to under one hundred, to the top ten books, you should take screen shots.

Take computer pictures once your book goes under the top one hundred and all the way to the top ten and number one. Do so for every country in which your book hits bestseller. When you hit number one (and anything under top one hundred in any of your categories) you are a verifiable #1 Amazon or International Best-Selling Author.

It's also great when a book continues maintaining its position as a bestseller. Categories are very important because where you place your book can influence who finds your book, who buys your book, and how your book sells. Some categories are easier than others because they have less congestion or competition. Self-help books are generally a difficult category, but placing your book in the appropriate category is significant in raising sales in one day. You want to see your book hit number one.

VIKI: I also suggest that it is the day of the sales and even more specifically it is a matter of how your book does hourly. Amazon takes rankings on an hourly basis and you know that, as Debbi has explained, Amazon does not keep a history of the ranking, so you have to take screen shots. As an author, analyze your book on an hourly basis. When you are promoting the book, it is truly wonderful because the book can become a bestseller in its category even if the previous hour it was not a bestseller.

It happens very quickly and it is really exciting. However, it is something you have to keep an eye on. You need to keep screen shots going as the book accelerates because unless you do, you will have no proof of your bestseller status. Taking screen shots as your book rises is one of the most critical points.

DEBBI: Yes, Amazon refreshes its ranking numbers every hour, so it is about being on top of your book's ranking hourly. If you were to do your own campaign, just know that you need to do this while being awake from 12:01 AM until midnight. Even better is to have a team doing this with you, and watching your book's numbers the days before and the days after the launch. Sometimes a book will continue accelerating and you'll want to stay on top of the life of your book if it continues to be a bestseller even after the book launch date. You'll need to have wide open days in order to do a great job during your launch, handling and managing every hour, watching the ranking numbers be refreshed, staying on top of your book, and remaining aware for when it hits and becomes number one.

When you reach bestseller, it's time to pop the champagne and celebrate. You have done it; you succeeded—make it fun and enjoy your success.

VIKI: It is interesting. Sometimes our books will hit bestseller in the middle of the night. We not only review U.S. rankings, but we review all of the other countries—we have to review all of the different countries as sometimes a bestseller happens for one hour in the middle of the night and then it drops down beyond number one bestseller in a category and never goes back up again. We have had this happen numerous times now and if we had not been reviewing the site hourly, we would have missed the top rating that it made.

It is very much an hourly monitoring situation to say nothing of the promotion that goes into making it happen beforehand.

DEBBI: The reason we keep our eyes reviewing the different countries and maintain a global view is that each Amazon country has its own website. The British Amazon website ends in .UK, Canada ends in .CA, and there's Spain and Italy and multiple international Amazon sites. Whenever and wherever you hit bestseller, grab it through a screen shot and have the proof that it happened. Sometimes your book is right up against authors and names that are very impressive.

In my case with my books, I was up against Sir Richard Branson and Don Miguel Luiz and Jack Canfield and other notables. Having a JPG photo of when my book was a bestseller above them is phenomenal to use for promotion.

You can send your bestseller photos out in many ways—put them on your website, send to social media and share with folks who have been supporting you.

AUTHOR: I have a question pertaining to self-help books and inspirational books. Are there any types of self-help, inspirational books that are more attractive? What messages do you find are more attractive for audiences? What are they looking for based on your experience?

VIKI: For me, the bottom line is that whatever your message is, it's going to attract the right people to your book. I would not conform any book to any type of formula. You definitely want to make your book readable and have it edited in a professional way so people will find it appealing. I am talking about the content that comes from your soul. That needs to be your unique message and you will find your audience. If you can include something timely, that can be a plus. I really do believe that everyone has their own story to tell and that story will attract people. Even with an anthology, which basically is a book of chapters on one topic written by numerous authors, anywhere from twenty people to over a hundred people submit chapters that become one book. What I love about an anthology is that everyone seems to find something in the book that really appeals to them. Some people may find one nugget that is going to change their lives and other people may find lots of nuggets in lots of chapters.

If someone tries to deter you from your message, remember the story of Jack Canfield when he and Mark Victor Hanson first wrote *Chicken Soup for The Soul*. They went to over one hundred forty-eight different publishers and were turned down. They approached a dear friend of mine, Rick Frishman, and he figured out a way to get them a deal. Rick was one of the top publishers around, and he was the one who basically put *Chicken Soup for the Soul* on the map when everybody they went to told them that their book format would never work. Jack and Mark were basically told the book format was just horrible, and that no one would read it, yet they sold the *Chicken Soup for the Soul* rights for millions and millions of dollars.

They followed their dreams and one of the things that Jack Canfield shared with us in an interview was that he and Mark Victor Hanson agreed to go around promoting their book. When everyone told them, "That book is not going to go anywhere," they kept putting in effort every day and finally got the one life-changing "yes."

I would say you do not want to go with trends to the level that it distorts your message; you want to keep your message pure. You also want to make sure that you have professional people around you to ensure your book is readable and appealing.

DEBBI: I interview people all the time. Many of people I interview are authors and I read the books of those I am going to interview before we go on air. I prepare for each guest and feel it is my responsibility to do so. I also love the fact that the author I'm about to meet offers a level of expertise about their subject. Since I read so many books constantly for interview guests and authors, I urge anyone writing with surety that it is important to express your unique message. How will your book stand out otherwise? Haven't you picked up a self-help or inspirational book and read it and thought that it is like everything else out there? There is a glut of books out there, so what will distinguish your book from everybody else's?

If a writer feels it is important to write, then say something different, and address what readers have not read before. What is your unique point of view, what is indigenous to you and only you that your past/path has created into wisdom that nobody else knows? Maybe it is humor or maybe it is a perspective or strategy. Whatever it is, make the material of your book all your own.

I have read so many of these books that it often seems to repeat the same stuff and is stale. Why not make your book like static electricity? Be riveting or make it new. What do you know that you can put out there that hasn't been said before and hasn't been expressed through your filter and through your distinctive perspective? Trust yourself. Don't try to be like anybody else, and you will be successful. Trust yourself and trust your voice.

Next, another word about editing your book. As I mentioned, I am the daughter of a professional editor and I often see mistakes in books. No matter how amazing your message is, having a book with typos and mistakes makes it entirely unprofessional and very distracting to read. It takes a book way, way down in its ranking and appeal. Pay somebody and have your book professionally edited—even if you think you got all the typos on your own, or through your friend who marked it up, believe me, you didn't find all the mistakes. Have your book edited by a professional and make it magnificent.

So those two things: invest in your book's unique message/trust your voice and hire a professional editor—that's the best advice I can give.

VIKI: I interview a number of *New York Times* best-selling authors and in addition to having a unique message, they do research and collaborate with other people in their work, and give them credit in their book. Although your message is unique, the foundation for your message may not be totally revolutionary. It can be the same information but organized in a unique way that is received differently.

When you bring people in and you give them credit in your book for their perspective and for what they have done, contact them, let them know you admire their work, and see what that might bring to you from their standpoint.

It is wonderful to look at your book as a collaboration of other experts on the subject. When you bring them in, it is amazing what can happen beyond what's just in your head and what's in your heart to a level of partnership that can be fruitful in so many ways.

DEBBI: Viki, what you are sharing is actually surreptitious. When I wrote my first book, *Dare to Dream: This Life Counts*, my intent was to share how to go after a goal and what the recipe is to pragmatically and inwardly seize the goal, no matter where you're starting from, and turn the dream into your actual life. To accomplish that, I wanted to break it up so I designed the book's contents like music, where there is a verse, the main body of the book, and then I added a bridge so the rhythm and information of the book was broken up in a positive and easily flowing way, which also created interest for the reader and depth. In music, the bridge is often used to contrast with and prepare for the return of the verse and the chorus in a song. My book was a song to my readers and to add the bridge in between chapters meant collaborating with other people to tell their specific stories of where they started, what their dream initially was, how they created their dream into reality, and what their life was like now. Men and women shared immensely moving and inspirational life stories—different people from various walks of life. So this is another variation on how you can collaborate in your book. The majority of my first book was in my voice, interspersed with real stories from real people. It flowed so well and had great reader impact.

My second book, *Wisdom to Success: The Surefire Secrets to Accomplish All Your Dreams*, was a surprise in that I actually had written another book entirely. I happened to be listening back to an interview I'd done, and hearing the information I shared in the interview I felt there was wisdom there that could be shared with others. I listened to many hours of me being interviewed (I have been on at least 800 shows as a guest expert), and I realized there was a book there. I paid someone to transcribe all of my interviews and after many, many edits, chapter changes, juxtapositions, and switches to make the book read well, work well and positively influence others, a best-selling book was born. That is something else available to you as well regarding collaboration. In each chapter of that second book was my voice and the voice of the radio host.

Collaborations are also great because the people you feature will get excited about being a part of the book and then often, subsequently will promote the book in a big way. When you have many collaborators that means many promotions to all new audiences and followers and databases. Most collaborators will market your book on their own due to their excitement about being involved and featured.

If you choose to collaborate, it sets up the book ultimately for the greatest win-win situation.

VIKI: I love that win-win; it is my favorite situation.

DEBBI: The readers win, those who are featured in your book win, and you stepping into your dream for your bestselling book is a win.

Viki, can you share any publishing success stories that would inspire me?

VIKI: We have taken over a thousand authors to bestseller and almost all of them have gone to number one international bestseller; the record has been incredible. We are thrilled that people have entrusted us with their work in order to make that happen.

One of my favorite books was a collection of stories from one hundred and one women who had gone through unimaginable things—everything from sexual abuse to physical and emotional trauma and other very trying situations. The authors shared what they had been through. Some of the stories were horrific, some simple, and some of the stories were about women who did not feel they were deserving or good enough to achieve their goals, which is something that you are such an expert in coaching people through, Debbi. (One of the benefits of this book is we definitely encourage you to do what you are meant to do in life.) In this anthology, these women went through so much and shared how they came out the other side. I did all the interviews myself, and I have to say that as a woman, that book touched me the most because it was incredible to witness the enormous changes people created in their lives.

What I really found mind-blowing was that some of the women whose stories weren't as dramatic were liked the most, and were the stories we got feedback on as really touching people's lives since they opened up and shared on a personal level.

You know I have really had a great life on every level from the day I was born, and I have experienced tremendous successes. I wanted to add something to the book and I thought, "I don't have anything dramatic to contribute." About six months before the book came out, when we were in the midst of the interviews I, who had always had a healthy life, who never even had colds, the flu, or anything, ended up with blood clots in my lungs and went to the emergency room in a drastic situation.

We live in a small community up in the mountains in New Mexico, and while in the local emergency room, the doctors said, "If we don't give you this treatment, you are going to die. If we give you this treatment, you might possibly have a stroke or have mental disabilities or it could kill you." It was basically a powerful blood thinner because the clots were blocking both my lungs. So my beloved Terry and I talked about worse case scenarios, and where everything was located in the house in case the worst actually happened. Then they administered this horrible drug to me. I don't take any drugs, ever, but obviously it worked. That horrible drug saved my life.

They airlifted me out to Albuquerque and I spent the next two weeks in ICU, and then I realized I had a story to tell. The interesting thing about this was that it wasn't the story about near death that was most touching; it was the revelation of how I developed new respect and hopefulness in a traditional medical community where previously I had been guarded and fearful. That revelation and what it did for me mentally and spiritually was my story, not that I almost died. Oftentimes our small stories where we reveal our raw emotions on even "little" topics have the greatest relevance.

DEBBI: Lives can change in a single moment, and from a mess we have lived through is often born our message.

VIKI: I worked with an author who was only comfortable wearing blue jeans and she wrote a book that included the story about her ability to accept herself without having to dress in Chanel or put on a designer suit in her professional speaking career.

Her story was about being able to present herself authentically through dressing in blue jeans, and that is one of the most powerful stories she wrote in a book. I guess the message here is that stories do not have to be earthshaking. My story was about a near-death situation, but the real content was the emotion that living it conjured up and my ability to overcome fear. I think for Christine, the blue jeans woman, it was about being able to be confident in who she is and what her preferences are. She was at our EIPPY book events to receive an award and when she got on stage to accept it, she was indeed wearing jeans. Some simple stories are more powerful than the dramatic happenings when sincere emotions are freely shared.

DEBBI: Absolutely! And we can resonate with these stories. When we are comfortable being ourselves, we are putting it out in our books and in the media through the filter of who we are. Allow people to see through to your essence and to align with everything you're putting out there. It is a terrific thing when you embrace who you really are, like the blue jeans lady, and let your proclivities shine out to the world. What we have experienced and lived through shapes us and our books. Viki, your story is inspirational and I am so glad you are okay and with us today. You have an important voice.

VIKI: Thank you so much. Regarding what we have lived through and what shapes us, it wasn't until I was in the helicopter being carted off and I was looking down through the glass floor in the helicopter that I thought, "I am on a gurney here and almost died, but this is not my time. I am going to live, I need to live, I have more to do, I have more to contribute." I made a decision to live and I share that because like you, Debbi, I have interviewed a lot of people. I do most of the interviews for books in addition to radio shows every week. Everyone that I have talked with who has had a near-death experience has told me that somewhere in the process they made a conscious decision to live.

For me, I can only say it was undeniable. I decided that living is what I wanted. Whether or not that was in agreement with the divine, I found that that is consistent with everyone else's near-death stories. With all of your dreams and desires—and you are the dream expert, Debbi—if you have that undeniable desire to be whatever you want to be, it can happen for you.

DEBBI: I agree. What an encouraging and moving way to leave you in this final chapter. If you have it in your heart to do a book, write it and then turn it into a bestseller. Give your book an afterlife because we know dreams can come true. My motto is, "Dreams are free, so free your dreams."

VIKI: I love that!

DEBBI: You have now learned about how to become a best-selling author and what goes into the process. You have also learned how you can utilize media, specifically radio, to promote and market your business and your book successfully. You now know the enormity of what's possible and how implementing this information can shift your lives, with some direction and strategy for where you desire most to go.

We look forward to your book becoming a bestseller, and to you being a best-selling author and parlaying all of that into being a PR Magnet. You deserve to be getting your message out on radio and in all the venues that are hungry for you and your very unique message.

I thank you from the bottom of my heart. Viki, it has been such an honor and pleasure to teach and collaborate with you in this book. I am grateful and I thank you, my friend.

VIKI: I thank you Debbi, and I thank everyone who has committed to join us on this journey. I wish you all the best and the door is open should you want to continue working with me and Debbi to make all your PR and bestseller dreams come true.

Discover More:
Become a Best-Selling Author and Radio PR Magnet
with Debbi and Viki in a comprehensive class:
<u>BookRadio.Expert</u>

About the Authors

If it has to do with messaging through books or radio—**Debbi Dachinger** is the Media Maven to get you there! Debbi is CEO of *Radio Mastery Training* (concierge level VIP coaching mediamasteryradio.com) for entrepreneurs, speakers and authors to accelerate skills (tech, strategy and private consulting) for media interviews; her clients become savvy and successful while getting big results from media interviews. She also runs the *Bestseller Launch Program* with products taking authors to international best-selling book status.

As founder of *Media Mastery Books and Radio*, Debbi has successfully prepared hundreds of media spokespersons. Her clients have included international speakers, best-selling authors, transformational leaders, entrepreneurs, CEOs, business women and men, physicians and financial gurus.

A veteran broadcast personality, Debbi has more than ten years of experience in American radio as well as a three decade-long entertainment career. She brings this firsthand media experience to every training session. Debbi's credits include 102.5 WLOQ, 1360 AM WNJC, LA Talk Radio, KOST 103.5 FM, WROM Detroit, and Huffington Post, Roku, YouTube as well as TV: FX, MTV and Lifetime. She produces and hosts an award-winning, syndicated radio show *"Dare to Dream,"* heard on 66 stations.

She is interviewed and speaks from stage as a Success and Media expert. She is a motivational speaker, was an award-winning actress and singer, and a professional voice-over artist. She was the keynote speaker at the *Women's Calgary Red Carpet* event; Global Influence Summit, the Business Success Summit, and was invited to present at the prestigious *Los Angeles Conscious Life Expo* as well as San Francisco's *New Living Expo* in the *Study of Achieving Dreams*, along with other distinguished speakers, including Marianne Williamson. She has been seen in the news, documentary films, on the cover of *One Magazine* and *EYDIS Magazine,* and is a contributor to *PUBLISHED! Magazine.*

Awards and Accolades: Editor's Pick: Featured Intriguing Creator, Broadcasting Industry Lifetime Achievement Award, an induction into the Who's Who Hall of Fame for Entertainment, Winner of Successful Achievements from Voices of Women Worldwide, recipient of Heart and Spirit Award from the Evolutionary Business Council.

Debbi is an international speaker with an inspirational video channel at: YouTube.com/debontheradio.

http://debbidachinger.com
http://MediaMasteryRadio.com
http://mybestsellerbook.com

Best-selling Books by Debbi Dachinger

- *Dare to Dream: This Life Counts!*
- *Wisdom to Success: The Surefire Secrets to Accomplish all your Dreams*
- She is also a contributor to 25 anthologies, including: *Reinvention, 30 Days to Social Media Success, My Creative Thoughts, My Big Idea Book, The Spirits and Stories of Trees, Big Dreams and Hard Work, The Essential Social Media Marketing Handbook,* and *Ready, Aim, Inspire!*

All titles are available on Amazon.

Viki Winterton is founder of Expert Insights Publishing, home of best-selling and award-winning books and magazines, where visionaries and those on the rise come together to create immediate impact.

Expert Insights Publishing is built on the solid foundation of over 30 years of expertise in promotion, publishing, product development, networking, and success. Fortune 100 companies and individuals across the globe know Viki for fostering powerful and loyal relationships and supporting her communities in wildly creative, unique, and wonderful ways.

Viki is also a multiple #1 international best-selling author and award-winning publisher, international speaker and media magnet, founder of Bestselling Authors International Organization, Write Now! Broadcast and Write Away, Write Now!, the global community where writers find everything they need at each stage of their journey.

ExpertInsightsPublishing.com

Viki's Companies:

The Agency
Bestselling Authors International Organization
Founder of Expert Insights Family of Opportunity:
Write Now, and Expert Insights Radio
The Coach Exchange Global Community
Bestseller Launchpad Web TV Broadcast
Write Away, Write Now! Learning Center
Expert Insights Publishing Bestseller Books
Expert Insights Publishing International Best-Selling Books
The Extravaganza and EIPPY Book Awards Events

Viki's #1 International Best-Selling Books:

Beyond Your Book
Cancer: From Tears to Triumph
My Big Idea Book
My Big Idea Workbook
My Creative Thoughts Journal
My Creative Thoughts Workbook
PR Magnet
Ready, Aim, Captivate!
Ready, Aim, Excel!
Ready, Aim, Impact!
Ready, Aim, Influence!
Ready, Aim, Inspire!
Ready, Aim, Soar!
Ready, Aim, Thrive!
Tail Waggin' Tales
Wounded? Survive! Thrive!!!

Viki's Award-Winning Magazines:

Insights
PUBLISHED!
Stress Free
Resources Uncovered

Viki's Award-Winning Videos:
https://www.youtube.com/playlist?list=PL5u0HomaUTodmBLJzBVE3DY6blFXTkT9R

Resources

Become a Best-Selling Author and Radio PR Magnet
with Debbi and Viki in a comprehensive class:
BookRadio.Expert

Bestseller Launchpad
bestsellerlaunchpad.com

Bestselling Authors International Organization
bestsellingauthorsinternational.org

Dare to Dream
debbidachinger.com

Dare to Dream Radio
debbidachinger.com/category/radio-interview-archives

Extravaganza and EIPPY Book Awards
MyBookAward.com

Free Insider Tips to be First-rate at Radio Interviews
debbidachinger.com

Get Known Now!
expertinsightspublishing.com/HowtoGetKnownNow.html

How to Be a Successful Radio Host
debbidachinger.com/want-to-be-a-radio-host

Media Mastery Expert Coaching
mediamasteryradio.com

PUBLISHED! Magazine
expertinsightspublishing.com/PUBLISHEDGift.html

Self-Publish to International Bestseller Audio Program
debbidachinger.com/author

Write Away, Write Now Global Community
writeawaywritenow.com

www.ingramcontent.com/pod-product-compliance
Lightning Source LLC
Chambersburg PA
CBHW071415180526
45170CB00001B/114